A
TIME
OF
OUR
LIVES

by

ETHEL KILGOUR

 City of Aberdeen

To Elizabeth, Jean, Margaret and Christine,
my daughters.

Thanks are due to:

The City of Aberdeen, Arts & Recreation Division.
City of Aberdeen Planning Department for the use of
photographic illustrations.

Project Editor: Michael Thomson
Project Co-ordinator: Jim Pratt

INTRODUCTION

There are many who will never have known the St Clements area of Aberdeen as anything other than a rather bleak industrial estate, deserted outwith business hours. But once, before its decline in the 1950s and 1960s and its clearance and wholesale demolition in the 1970s, it was a bustling working-class hive of activity with streets of tenements, shops, a school, and people - people among whom I grew up.

I was born in 1922, four years after the end of the 'war to end wars', during which almost a generation of this country's manhood went to its death in the mud of France and Belgium. Survivors came home, many broken in health, to find little hope of obtaining work in the depressed post-war years. Matters improved as the 1920s went on, but when the disastrous Depression of 1929 brought industry to a standstill there was great suffering, not the least in St Clements, where the shipyards had provided a livelihood for much of the population, and where for many the period between the two wars was one of social deprivation, unemployment, poverty and poor housing.

Our family was not the worst off, but neither was it well off, and we too knew some hard times as the number of mouths to feed increased. That, however, was only one aspect of life in those times. This book is an attempt to convey some varied glimpses of the area as seen through my eyes during my childhood and teens. Inevitably it is centred around home and family, but I have also attempted to capture the atmosphere of the times by looking a little beyond the immediate confines of St Clements. No doubt those who lived through this period have many memories of their own, but for younger generations, here are a few impressions of what it was like to live in a now much changed quarter of Aberdeen at a time not so very long ago, but such a world away.

CHAPTER 1
THE 1920s – A ST CLEMENTS FAMILY

St Clements lies between Aberdeen harbour and Old Fittie, with which it has always been popularly linked, although its character was quite diffent. Fittie was built at the turn of the nineteenth century to replace an even older fishing village, whereas the growth of St Clements accompanied the city's industrial expansion in the course of the century, its location giving it a strongly maritime bias. It housed a large population, typically of large families crammed into two-room flats in eight to ten-flat Victorian tenements with outside toilets, wash-houses in the 'backies', and often with only a single communal black iron cold water sink tucked in a corner of the stair landing as water supply.

The 'main street' of St Clements ran from the top of Church Street to Wellington Street and Messrs. Russell's (later Hall Russell's) shipyard gates. Officially it was named St Clement Street, but to us it was 'The Tarrie', being the only macadamed thoroughfare in the area. On one side was St Clements Street School, and on the other St Clement's Church. A maze of streets – Lime Street, Clarence Street, Church Street, Wellington Street – led to the the dockland area, while on the other side was the beach and the sea. Beyond the shipyards, the river Dee flowed into the sea between the North and South piers. Further South was Old Torry, and to the East was the unique seafaring and God-fearing enclave of Fittie where the people spoke their own variant of the Aberdeen vernacular and considered the denizens of St Clements to be uptowners or 'Toonsers'. Very territorially-minded, they would not even let us walk on their beach. Their houses were solid and defensive, built in squares to ward off the ferocity of winter gales and the high seas which crashed by their walls.

Running northward from St Clement Street was Links Street, a long narrow thoroughfare with tenements along the east side, and on the west a single corner block (No.1) with the St Clements Bar incorporated into it. Next to the bar was St Clement's church hall, then a woodyard and a fish curing works. As its name suggests, the street led to the grassy Links. It was sometimes known as 'The Jungle', because it had a reputation as being a rough area, but I am certain that this was not the case during the 1920s and early 1930's; I was born and spent my childhood at No. 2 Links Street, a matching corner block opposite the St Clements Bar and above Jock Wood's licensed grocery shop.

The only granite houses in Links Street were those on the corners. The rest were built of brick and were known as 'the brickers'. Although not as substantial as granite buildings, they were still quite good except for those comprising numbers 4, 6 and 8. Dim, dingy, poorly built and crumbling, these three tenements had no facilities at all – not even washhouses or drying spaces behind them. Clothes had to be washed in zinc baths in the backies and dried in the rooms, with all the resultant health risks. The dark lobbies were painted in a chalky ochre, a cheap material which rubbed off on one's clothes.

A little research brings to light the reason for the presence of those two distinct sets of 'brickers'. The St Clements area was laid out in the early 19th century, and the poorer 'brickers', which are shown on the first Ordnance Survey map, drawn in the 1860s, may well have dated from that time. From the 1850s, the site of the northern part of Links Street was covered by the St Clements Chemical Works of Mr William Rattray, a large-scale manufacturing chemist who had begun as an apothecary in the Woolmanhill and Schoolhill area 30 or more years previously. Early on, his brother Robert had joined him as an apothecary, but had shortly after joined the staff of the Royal Infirmary, where he (Robert) worked his way up to the post of surgeon and eventually Superintendent. William Rattray's name disappears from local directories as of 1880, and just at that time plans were drawn up in the name of Robert Rattray to redevelop the Chemical Works site for housing. In the drawings, which still survive, it was proposed to separate by gates the new development from the rest of the street. The houses were completed in 1882, and Robert Rattray retired the following year, but he lived only until 1885. He did at least leave behind some decent artisan housing that was very desirable when compared with its miserable neighbours – which, for all that, survived until after the second World War.

Returning to our corner house, one half of the tenement faced Links Street and the other (with our kitchen in it) the Tarrie. Corner windows gave a good view of both streets, and our tiny bedroom overlooked the backies. All of the families at No. 2 were longstanding tenants whose children had grown up there, and with the exception of one other child I and my brothers and sisters were the only youngsters. Across the street at No. 1 the situation was much the same, although in one of the small two-room flats there lived a family with eight children ranging from baby to teenager, and in another lived two small children with their young mother, who had lost an arm in an accident but still managed to wield a scrubbing brush and floor cloth diligently. The houses in that area were owned by private landlords who would seldom willingly let a large family move in, but St Clements still teemed with children, William's Square off Garvock Wynd and Yeats Lane off Miller Street being particularly congested.

The flat in which I was born was on the first floor of No. 2 Links Street, reached by two flights of wooden stairs with a landing and large window between them. It had only two rooms, kitchen and bedroom. The kitchen was quite large, with a window sink (this window overlooked the Tarrie), a mahogany sideboard, a bed, a French-polished chest of drawers, an easy chair, and a table covered in shiny American oil-cloth – a material very widely used for such purposes. The fireplace was finished in black and steel. On brackets under the mantel-shelf was a thick brass rod with an embroidered cloth pelmet attached to it by brass tacks. This rod was a fixture on most house fireplaces, and in addition to performing a decorative function it came in very useful as a support for drying small articles of clothing! The bedroom was so small that it only just held a full-size bed. Its window faced eastwards, and on cold still winter nights we could hear the roar of the sea.

On the other side of the landing was the three-room flat of my grandparents, quite a typically appointed dwelling of the time. The kitchen was fitted with a window sink and a black and steel fireplace like ours. It also contained a recessed bed draped with side curtains, a dresser and a kitchen table. Next to the sink was a food cupboard, and to the right of the sink was a gas cooker. The penny gas meter was under the food cupboard, the door of which was sawn in half to give easy access. In the opposite corner was my grandfather's easy chair, placed comfortably behind the door, away from draughts. On the mantel shelf stood a pair of china dogs, two brass candlesticks and a tea caddy. Above it was a curved brass gas-bracket on a swivel, a mirror and a framed studio photograph of my grandmother in a long, flowing, high-necked Edwardian dress. She was shown sitting on a chair, holding a baby – my mother, who was born in 1903.

Along the hallway was a small bedroom with a dressing chest, a wardrobe, and a bed in a recess. In front of the bed was a mat – apart from that, the floor was covered entirely in linoleum. The front room had two windows (one of which was on the corner) with white-painted frames and sills. In this room was a piano, a wardrobe with a mirrored door, a large moquette easy chair, a china cabinet and a beautiful tall chest of drawers made of red mahogany. On top of the chest of drawers was a glass case containing a model of the Cutty Sark in full sail, one of over fifty ship models superbly crafted by my grandfather. The china cabinet, also made by my grandfather, sat beside the corner window. Among the treasured articles that it contained were two fine china tea-sets and a 1901 Edward VII Coronation mug in pristine condition. Also by the window was a polished wooden plant stand with an aspidistra in a brass holder. There was a bed in the corner, and in the centre of the room was a small low table. The fireplace (which had a mat in front of it) was of marble, and inside the brass kerb was a long vitreous enamel plate which prevented hot coals from falling out. Hearth plates were then very common – they came in various colours and patterns, and were easily cleaned with a cloth.

On one wall of the front room was a pictorial impression of Jesus; on another was a framed photograph of my mother, shown wearing a soft collar and with her hair coiffured in ringlets. There was also a photograph of the trawler *Star Of Liberty*, on which my father had been a crew member on a trip to Germany. (I remember that he brought me back a china mama-doll for which he had paid only 2s.11d. – 25 pence now. Germany's economy was in such chaos that goods were very cheap for us – the same doll cost 25 shillings in Singer Sewing Machine Shops in this country!)

A third flat on our landing, similar to my grandparents', was occupied by a grown-up family by the name of Rennie, who looked after their long-widowed mother, a quiet gentle woman. On the next floor lived the Browns, the Riddels and a Mrs Craib with her daughter Jean. Above were two attic rooms and a drying loft. Everyone took a turn at scrubbing the stairs, which were kept very clean and always retained the slightly carbolic smell of Kilty soap. The stairway was lit by a paraffin lamp fixed to one of the walls, and turns were taken in keeping the lamp fuelled and its glass globe cleaned.

On the left of the stone-floored downstairs lobby, in two small rooms, lived Beldie Clouder and her frail, ageing parents. Beldie was about 18, and was a stocky, buxom, energetic young woman with reddish gold hair and a somewhat florid complexion, always cheery and usually singing as she wielded the scrubbing brush; her kitchen was always spotless. Everyone knew and liked Beldie – some said (in a kindly way) that she had 'a tongue that would clip cloots', for she loved to blether with folk, especially when the subject was Bing Crosby, whose rendition of 'Where The Blue Of The Night Meets The Gold Of The Day' was one of the great hits of the early 1930s. She was so star-struck over Bing that she once asked my mother if I could accompany her to the Cinema House in Skene Terrace (a good way off) to see one of his films. Permission was granted, and I enjoyed the change from our usual local cinemas, the Star and the Casino, while to Beldie, Bing was a real 'sheik' and a 'rare crooner'.

The St Clements Bar, with its gleaming brass rails and cuspidors, was the local venue for those men in the street who could afford a drink. At closing time (9 o'clock) on Saturday nights the men would come out three sheets to the wind and be greeted by the kids with shouts of 'Gie's a penny, mister'. Coppers would be thrown in the air, and a mad scramble would ensue. On occasion, I was sent over to the bar with a tall china jug to fetch two pennyworth of stout. Grandma, who otherwise strongly disapproved of drink, would carefully put a red hot poker into the stout and then add sugar to produce a frothy sweet liquid which she maintained was good for us, and of which we would all be given a cupful.

Huge drays drawn by Clydesdale horses carried fish, usually large cod, along Links Street from the market to the curing-house for drying. The smell lingered long after the cart had passed, especially in summer. The road-spraying wagon(also horse-drawn) was a welcome attraction for children as it sprayed water on to the street from a tank at the rear. To the Cleansing Department this may have been merely a means of laying the dust on a hot summer day, but to us it was a most enjoyable diversion as, barefoot, we followed the cart.

The church of St Clement had two gates and two paths through the churchyard. That on the right led to the Session House where mothers' meetings, choir practices, etc, were held until 1930 when the church hall was built next door to the St Clements Bar. We children watched the hall take shape brick by brick that summer. At last, the harling was applied and the workmen hoisted into place above the entrance a polished granite tablet bearing the year of the hall's construction. The Sunday School held a Grand Christmas Party that year, in advance of which auspicious occasion I was taken by my mother to 'Raggie' Morrison's drapery store in George Street to buy material for a party dress. For 6d. a yard (two and a half pence) we obtained some nice blue silky cloth which was soon made up on our old sewing machine. My mother was completely self-taught as a dressmaker, but not for nothing was she known as having 'good hands'.

That first Christmas party in the new hall was a great success, and I felt like a princess in my new blue dress, especially when my Granny declared that I would be 'The belle o' the ball'. We were subject to just one restriction – the girls had to wear soft slippers and the boys their 'jimmies' so as not to damage the new wooden floor!

My grandparents were John Masson, from the Fittie squares, and Margaret Brack Masson. Living with them were my great-grandmother Jane Brack, my aunt Daisy (aged 16 when I was born) and my young uncles Andrew and George aged eight and five respectively. Great-grandfather Brack, who died before I was born, had, of course, also lived there. A one-time whaler, he, together with his family, had travelled widely with the herring fleet. He was a boss, a weighman, and Jane had worked at herring-gutting, as had her sisters. For a time they had lived in Shetland, but moved as far south as Great Yarmouth, later settling in Aberdeen. My grandmother once told me that she attended school in Shetland, and that Jane had been born in Eyemouth. Jane Brack died when I was four years old. She was greatly missed, having looked after the household in order to allow Grandmother to resume work at the fish, and she had spoiled Andrew and George very much, showering them with love as well as gifts of pennies from her apron pocket.

John Masson was born and bred in the house built for his father William Masson at 19 North Square. Like most Fittie folk, William Masson had been a man of the sea – a brass plate on his door read 'William Masson, Pilot'.

Those were brave hardy souls, who faced the fury of the North Sea in their fishing boats. The women of the village also worked hard, shelling hundreds of mussels and baiting the fishing lines for their men very early in the morning before readying their children for school. It was a gruelling life, full of uncertainties, never knowing when the lifeboat would have to be launched into a stormy sea to aid a stricken vessel.

The neat clean village of Fittie had (and still has) a unique character. Some of the houses are of only a single storey, tucked alongside neighbours which have been rebuilt and extended to all heights – one in North Square, taller than all the rest, is to this day known as 'The Tower Of Babylon'. Built of granite and displaying a great variety of architecture, they adjoin one another in rows, forming the squares. Some, mainly the single-storey ones, have very small windows. There used to be no inside plumbing or sinks, only a well with a cold water tap for each row, but now this quaint old place enjoys 'all mod cons' while still retaining its historic identity.

In the centre of North Square stands the Mission Hall where for generations the people of Fittie have joined in their favourite hymns and choruses. In front of the houses (not behind them, as is the usual domestic arrangement), stand outhouses of all shapes and sizes; only a few are modern replacements. A ship's bell, a ship's wheel and other relics decorate the little pieces of garden in front of the varicoloured painted sheds, mementos of the past.

Near the long concrete North Pier stands the 19th century Round House from which customs men once hailed the passing ships, shouting through a megaphone 'Where are you bound?' to those leaving port, and 'Where are you from?' to those arriving. Now it too has been modernised with radar equipment, so essential to all ships at sea.

This was the place where my grandfather John Masson was born. At the tender age of 10 he was apprenticed as a carpenter aboard his father's trawler *Kittywake*, and he never to my knowledge spent a day off work through illness. Similarly tough and hardworking was my Grandmother. When, once, she took an attack of sciatica, it was to her infinite disgust that she was obliged to remain in bed. Grandfather's adventures at sea were many and full of danger. An account of some of them was related in an article in the 'People's Journal' in 1949. For this he was photographed holding one of the products of his consuming hobby – the building of model ships. The precision that he attained showed him to be a first-rate craftsman, his favourite model being that of the trawler *Danestone*. He would spend the long winter nights painstakingly working away, often ankle deep in wood shavings, until the object of his labour was finished, painted and beautiful. The care that he took with the smallest detail was infinite; even the ship's number and name would be picked out in tiny letters. He hardly ever wore glasses, although he did possess a pair which he bought from Woolworth's. They would be put on only for the completion of finer points.

In addition to making models purely for display, he turned his hand to making a few small working fishing boats which he named after members and friends of the family, so the *Margaret*, the *Daisy* or the *Nellie* could be seen out on the sea with Andrew, George and their friends aboard. These boats, despite their small size, were equipped with an engine, maintained by Andrew. With one exception, they were built after my grandfather had retired and moved with Grandmother to a room in the house in which he was born, and in which by that time other members of the family were living. This move was made mainly on economic grounds – even in the early years of the second World War £1 a week each was a poor pension for a married couple.

Grandfather's woodworking capabilities seemed limitless. He made for Georgie and myself a wonderful hobby-horse with wheels and pedals; on this we rode slowly and proudly up and down the street. We had lots of wooden toys, a doll's cradle, and a pram, most of which were still in use when my own eldest daughter was born.

My grandparents always had a dog, which Grandfather would walk on the sands to the Don and back, but dog-walking was not for Sundays. The Sabbath was strictly observed, winter Sundays being spent quietly reading either a book of Border Tales or a large book of Bible stories. The wireless and other sources of music remained silent, no Sunday papers were allowed, and no whistling of 'sangs' was permitted. It was indeed the Sabbath as Grandfather had been brought up to know it in Fittie.

Ironically, it was the sea that indirectly caused John Masson's death. Walking on the sands on a 'coorse' day, he was drenched by a large wave and had to walk all the way back to North Square in that state. This brought on a severe bout of pneumonia, and although at one point he recovered enough to ask the doctor whether he could smoke his pipe (!), he later had a relapse and died at an age well in excess of 80 years. Footnote: One day I asked him, 'Granda, fit wye are you aye singing 'A Farmer's Boy'?' He answered, 'Weel, I aye wanted t' ging oot to California an' hae a fairm'!

My name was chosen, my mother told me, after she read a novel by Ethel M. Dell around the time that I was born. I was never ecstatic about it – I would have preferred my mother's name Elizabeth or my grandmother's, Margaret. Granny herself was none too pleased, but was placated when my sister was named after her. A friend across the way in No. 1 Links Street had sisters Daisy and Ruby, and also in the street lived the Sangster sisters Pansy and Violet – very colourful compared with 'Ethel', I thought, but I contented myself by thinking of the old saying 'What's in a name?'

In Old Fittie, people were often given by-names, I suppose to distinguish families in which names were handed down through generations. My father James McInnes was, to his amusement, described as 'Rachles'-Jock's-Lizzie's-Jim', 'Rachles' having been Great-Grandfather Masson's by-name. Fittie folk apparently liked to prefix their names with their maternal or paternal ones in a sort of instant 'Who's Who'!

On winter evenings when gales raged around the chimney tops, we would sit in my Granny's kitchen while she and my mother busily knitted jerseys and sea-boot stockings from thick black and white oiled wool. The gas light above the mantelpiece would flicker in the draught and sometimes the women would murmur 'Oh what a nicht – I wonder where aboot on the sea they are', 'they' being anyone that was out on the high seas, but in particular my father and my uncle Andy, out on the trawlers.

Those trawlers, the rusty, frail-looking coal-fired 'Smoky Joes', took their ten-man crews to the Faroes, Greenland and Iceland, braving the worst seas and the most terrible weather. My father was cook on one of them, having been lucky enough to obtain the job despite possessing no trawling experience. At the age of 14 he had driven a horse and cart from his home town near Glasgow to the fruit market in that city. When the first World War broke out, he volunteered (at the age of 17) for the Army and found himself in France with the Gordon Highlanders, working once again with horses, drawing limbers to the Front. Peacetime army service took him to India, but he returned to Aberdeen and was stationed at Castlehill Barracks.

The Barracks looked for all the world like a castle, towering above Justice and Commerce Streets. It was vacated when the Army moved to Bridge Of Don in 1935, and now a multi-storey housing complex stands in its place, but at that time on still summer nights we could hear from our house in Links Street the distant bugle sounding 'Lights Out'. While in Aberdeen, my father resigned his post and came home, bringing with him his Gordon tartan kilt which, in the hands of an expert seamstress, Mrs Stephenson, who lived in Wellington Street, provided kilts for myself, my sister and my brother James!

Desperate for a job, my father went to sea. He once told me that he was sea-sick for months, beginning as soon as the boat passed the North Pier, but if that was the case it did not stop him from gaining a first-class reputation for his cooking and for 'keeping a clean ship'. His army service had taught him everything that he knew, and it stood him in great stead. He was so highly rated in the trawling community that in 40 years he was never without work except when ill, and taxis would be sent to pick him up when it was time to leave – something otherwise unheard of.

Trawlermen worked on open decks in wild seas and freezing weather, gutting fish for hours on end after the boards came up, seven days a week

In the Barrack Square, Castlehill 1928.

Unloading the coal boat by use of the grab-bucket.

Labourers show how it was done in the good old-fashioned way.

Salvage operations on the wreck of the trawler "George Stroud", March 1936

for perhaps two or three weeks, and suffering salt water boils on their skin despite heavy jerseys, oilskins and sea-boots. When fishing in the freezing waters of the Faroes, Iceland and Greenland, they had an added enemy – ice, which formed on the rigging and on every part of the deck, and which had to be continually hacked at to clear it for the safety of the crew and to prevent the ship's capsizing through top-heaviness. All sleeping and eating were done in the foc'sle, the food being cooked on a coal-fired stove in a tiny galley near the stern. How my father did it I don't know, but he even managed to make bread and cakes – and I know the bread was good because he sometimes brought some home. Hard gruelling work called for good nourishing food, but crewmen had to pay for it all out of their wages. A high food bill at the end of a trip brought grumbles from the men, but the only alternative was insufficiency, so the cook's job was a rather unenviable one. Cooks were not the most highly paid crew members, so it was usual for them to act as part-time 'deckies', gutting fish in between making meals. A skipper who really valued his cook would not let him gut, but nevertheless a much harder life I cannot imagine. Tragedies at sea brought loss and sadness, and after all the rigours and hazards of a trip it was not uncommon to find large Icelandic ships so glutting the market with their enormous catches that prices tumbled and the hard-won Aberdeen fish went for nothing more than fish-meal.

My father once told me that he particularly dreaded sailing in the Pentland Firth, which he considered to be the most dangerous area of all, with its mountainous waves – 'Great lumps of water', he would say. Nevertheless, desperate situations (as he put it) required desperate measures, and trawler work became a way of life; it was either that or the poverty and soul-destroying idleness of the 'Broo'.

Even time in port was limited. The ship would dock in perhaps the late evening. My father would come home for a couple of hours' sleep, then back to the Fish Market to assist the lumpers in getting the fish out of the hold and ready for the morning sales. Home to bed again, then up and out for 'settling' at about 1 p.m. the next day. I remember this well, as I sometimes accompanied my father when he went to meet the skipper and crew in the back room of a bar in South Market Street. They sat around a large table, some with their pints of beer, and the pay was distributed. This included a share of the 'liver money' or 'cumshaw' as my father called it, which was the proceeds from the sale of the refuse from fish-gutting, put into sacks by the men to sell for processing into fish by-products. I think my father earned about six shillings a day, plus a bass bag of fish. Food expenses were deducted, a time set for sailing the following day, and the 'settling' was finished. In parting, I would be given a few pennies by the men to buy sweeties.

Next, my father would go to Rix's grocery on Commercial Quay to order stores for the next trip. He would sit on a chair by the counter, blethering a while with Mr and Mrs Rix before placing his orders. The rest of his time was then his own.

South Market Street in those days was a great hub of activity. Great Clydesdale horses pulled drays of fish boxes and coal, the unloading of which from the coal boats seemed to go on unceasingly, raising clouds of dust. It was a busy, noisy scene with the smell of fish strong in the air, greeting passengers as they alighted from trains at the Joint Station nearby. The strong, handsome horses clopped over the cassies, the carters expertly steering them and their heavy loads through the mass of traffic. Wordie's, the large Aberdeen firm of hauliers to which many of the animals belonged, was a name that everybody knew, and among the 'Knock Knock' jokes popular at that time was one which ran :
'Knock knock.'
'Who's there?'
'Ena!'
'Ena who?'
'Ena Wordie's horses!'
Steam-driven traction engines and lorries rumbled about the streets, the driver sitting in a little cabin which must have been stiflingly hot from the fire which burned behind a little door very close to him. 'Fit a rick it mak's', folk would say as the smoke belched out of the chimney. Many would sooner have had the horses!

I would walk hand in hand with my father from South Market Street to Guild Street, and into the Tivoli Theatre (neither the cinema nor the Beach Pavilion held any attraction for him). There he booked seats for the family at the first house that evening. We would then make our way back to Links Street via Regent Quay, and I would be bought coloured comics in a newsagent-cum-fancy goods shop at the bottom of Commerce Street. 'Sunbeam' was the expensive comic, costing all of twopence, and once I was also bought a paper parasol (only we called them 'sunshades'!) My father's wages were anything but good for the work that he did, but they were still far, far better than the Broo or Parish pittance which was the lot of so many who could not work for health reasons, or who simply could not find employment.

With trawl crews away in the fishing grounds for two or three weeks at a time, apprehension would set in at home as the days went by. Families made regular evening trips across the quays to the Fish Market, which, although closed, still had displayed outside it on Commercial Quay an ordinary school slate on which were written the names of ships that had docked late. The slate was scanned anxiously, but so often only the word

16

'overdue' was to be seen. Perhaps such anxiety was unfounded, but the sea takes away so many of those who make their livelihood on its dangerous waters. I remember when the trawler *Venetia* went down in 1933 – 'All Hands Lost', said the banner headlines, and the whole community was saddened. Then on Christmas eve 1935 the *George Stroud*, which had been to Methil for coal and had a scratch crew aboard, sank as it came into the channel between the North and South Piers, so near to safety. Three of the five-man crew were drowned within sight of people standing on the shore, powerless to help.

After one particularly gruelling trip, my father came home tired and morose, saying that he was sick of trawling. This was the first time that I had ever heard him complain, but the sea had been mountainous, the fo'csle had flooded, soaking bunks and floor, and the task of cooking in the galley (always difficult) had been made a nightmare. Father was determined to try for a job on shore, but the 'roaring twenties' had by then been succeeded by the 'hungry thirties' and many years were to pass before he achieved this aim. Happily, he did eventually obtain a job with the Town Council's Roads Department. He took a keen interest in bowling and gardening, which he did excellently – this from a man who had spent so much of his life at sea, and who had had so little home life for so long.

CHAPTER 2
CHARACTERS AND THE TARRIE

As I grew old enough to go out and mix with other children, I became aware of some of the characters of the area. 'Cheat-The-Hangman' was an odd soul who lived in the mean tenement at No. 4 Links Street. How he came by his nickname I do not know. He had tattered cauliflower ears, a bashed-in nose, rheumy eyes and cropped grey hair. Always attired in an old grey jacket and trousers and a dirty muffler, he would clump through the streets in heavy tacketty boots. His only company in his single room was his many cats, the urinal smell of which pervaded the immediate area. Tormented by the local kids, he must have led a miserable life. Around Guy Fawkes night, boys would poke bangers into his keyhole and yell 'Cheat-The-Hangman!' as they lit the fuse and ran away. Kids would shout at him in the street, and he would sometimes shake his fist and shout back, but he was completely harmless.

Far more sinister to us in our innocent little world was a small woman known as 'Cacky Apie' (or Eppie). I still see in my mind's eye her unkempt, frizzy brown hair above a brown weather-beaten face, and her shabby brown coat which reached to her broken, dirty brown shoes. Weird and wizened, she carried an old accordion bedecked with dirty ribbon streamers, and as she squeezed a few asthmatic, discordant notes from the instrument she usually got a halfpenny or two from the good-hearted people of the tenements. This strange woman with the equally strange, uncomplimentary name did no harm to anyone, but we were all afraid of her, and bairns who wouldn't go to sleep at night were threatened with the words 'I'll get Cacky Apie tae ye if ye dinna sleep'. This from otherwise loving, but weary, mothers.

There always seemed to be vendors in our street, scraping a living from our pennies and ha'pennies. For many years 'Luigi' was a familiar figure over the summer months when he would take up his stance with his ice cream cart (a small two-wheeled push-barrow) outside the St Clements Bar. Luigi was, as his name implies, an Italian – one of many who came to Britain at that time to sell ice cream or chips, or hot chestnuts in the winter. He was a short, stockily built man with the swarthy skin of his Mediterranean race. On most days he wore a neat white cotton coat, and he always wore a cloth cap. A cheery, friendly little character, he was well regarded by everybody. His barrow was ornate, with his name emblazoned on it in bright red and white scrolls. The top of the barrow, or counter, was painted white and was kept scrupulously clean. He seemed always to be wiping it with a clean cotton net cloth.

Luigi served up the most delicious ice cream cones (or 'cappies'), plain

A typical ice-cream vendor, 1928.

The corner of Wellington Street and St. Clement Street in the 1960's. A typical corner shop.

sliders, double sponges and chocolate sliders. The ice cream was made to his own recipe, and was quite unlike any other. Topped with raspberry juice it tasted marvellous. He could speak very little English, but the words that he did manage came out in broad Aberdonian! We children called him 'Lookie', which was much easier on the tongue than a foreign name like Luigi. In late afternoons when the ice around his freezer had melted, he would pull the large cork stopper from the vessel and would let us catch the cold water on our bare feet before it disappeared down the brander. When I was just a little girl, not yet at school, I used to ask Lookie for a cappie, without having the necessary halfpenny (or 'maik') to pay for it. Such was the trust between him and my father that when my father came in from sea, Lookie had only to say that 'Etelee' had had three or four cappies or whatever, and he would be paid without question.

Lookie disappeared at about the time when I left Links Street in 1934, and I discovered thereafter that the ice cream shop on Regent Quay was selling a very similar product to the distinctive and delicious one that had previously come from his barrow. I wondered if perhaps he had sold his recipe and retired home to sunny Italy – I certainly liked to think so.

'Full Friday' was another Italian ice cream man, with a stance at the Links end of Garvock Wynd, next to the gasworks. He too had a small barrow, but it looked very dull in comparison with Luigi's. How his title came to be inflicted on him I don't know, but the word 'full', being Aberdeen vernacular for 'foul', certainly carries connotations about cleanliness. Friday was a lean, sad-looking man, who always wore a brown trilby hat and a cotton coat. I used to think that perhaps he had a longing to be back in Italy rather than selling ice cream on a cold Scottish North East coast. At a party I once heard a song about Full Friday, part of which ran:

'Great big cappies up-a-ky,
Nothing inside – he's nae half fly,
Och aye, och aye............'

There were lots of other verses, all quite hilarious and all no doubt equally unfair to someone that I remember as a quiet, patient man.

The cry of 'Candy Bell' announced the arrival of a lady who sold sweets from a large four-wheeled, flat-topped wooden barrow. This caused considerable excitement among the children and gave rise to pleas to Ma for a ha'penny, with end results ranging from a bag of delicious boiled sweets for some to a slap on the lug for others! Candy Bell's sweets were all made in her own little factory. There were strippet balls, brandy balls, pear drops, cough drops, winter mixture and many other varieties, and the smell of fresh candy was mouth-watering. A maik bought a little bag of about six sweeties, while offers to help push the barrow were usually accepted with good grace and were rewarded with a free sweetie to suck. Needless to say, there was usually plenty of competition to lend a hand.

Candy Bell was fair-haired, of medium build and rather thin. She was very good-natured towards the kids, who were very choosy as to what they spent their precious ha'pennies on.

Another cry often heard in the street was that of 'Dulse' from the fish-wife, who sold this highly nourishing edible seaweed from a creel basket on her back. Her dress was typical of the period—blue striped heavy cotton skirt, voluminous and reaching to her ankles, and a woollen shawl around her shoulders, crossed at the front then tied at the back. When she appeared I would usually be sent out with a soup plate into which, for a penny, she would put a large helping of dulse. My mother would heat the poker in the fire until red hot, then press it on to the dulse, which made a loud crackling sound. A sprinkling of vinegar was added, then we all delved in. The seaweed's iodine content was undoubtedly good for us, but then my granny always maintained that anything brought from the sea was clean and good. She would encourage us to eat our fish with the words 'It'll gie ye brains', and considering my father's occupation we should have been brainy indeed!

A coal-man with a horse and cart would come along Links Street shouting 'Coal, two shillings a bag, coal!'. We loved the horses and would feed these hard-working, gentle animals with pieces of stale bread. A cart came round every day with urns of milk and some cream and eggs. The milkman would measure out the milk from a tap on the urn (it cost about 2d. a pint) and then transfer it into the buyer's jug. 'Straight from the coo', he would say. There was also a vegetable cart, the man walking beside the horse and calling, 'Balls o' meal tatties' at the top of his voice.

Periodically, the shout went up of 'The organ grinder mannie's here', and kids from the Links Street tenements ran to greet a man pushing what looked like a pianola on wheels. He took up his stance outside the bar, and the music would pour out as he turned a handle on the instrument. Its melodious tinkling sound was agreeable to listen to and for the children to dance to, and a small crowd would gather to hear 'Lily Of Laguna', 'Oh, Oh, Antonio', 'Daisy Bell', 'Oh You Beautiful Doll' and war-time tunes which were still popular. The man, an Italian named Benedetto Suave, smilingly acknowledged the coppers thrown to him from the tenement windows as he kept the music going, turning the handle with one hand and then the other. I think all the vendors and organ grinders knew that they would get a copper or two from Links Street; the people in those tenements had little enough money, but they had warm compassion for those with even less.

The organ grinder's music came as a pleasant interlude, enjoyed by everyone, as very few in 1920s St Clements had a gramophone and we did not know of anyone who had a wireless set until late in the decade or early in the next. Until then it was crystal sets only. My grandmother was one of those who did possess a gramophone, one of the old wind-up type with a heavy square base and a large fluted horn, on which were the words 'His Master's Voice' and the famous picture of the little dog. A small square tin of His Master's Voice needles was kept in a drawer close by. The 78 r.p.m. records were thick and heavy, yet so brittle that they had to be very carefully handled. At the end of each record, the motor had to be rewound by means of a handle in the side of the base. Andrew and George – just schoolboys then – enjoyed playing records, and also experimented with a crystal set on which they could hear through earphones, if only faintly, broadcasts from London. They knew all the tunes of the time ('the latest', as they would say) played by the top bands, but we younger children, especially the girls, preferred to dance and skip to the organ-grinder's happy sound. It made a nice change from our street games.

Opposite 'Cheat-The-Hangman' in the downstairs lobby of No. 4 Links Street was the tiny one-room shop of Maggie Caie, run jointly with her sister Bell (Bella). They were not rushed off their feet, but there were occasions when customers had to be served with coal (usually a quarter stone at a time) or paraffin by the bottle from a cellar in the backie, so someone had to be present in the shop. Weights and scales were used to carefully measure out the coal for the customer. I think four old pence was the price for a pailful.

The shop was so small that the counter was nothing more than a flap of wood, but Maggie sold all kinds of goods – pies (hot and cold), sweets, biscuits, bread, penny packets of tea (very popular), soap (Kilty brand), Hudsons washing powder, Monkey Brand abrasive, kindling sticks, and a host of other things. One could buy gas mantles there, and also in due course dry batteries for radios, returning the old ones for recharging. Of the variety of odours which met the customer on entering the shop, probably the most pervasive was that of the kindling, which gave off a strong resinous smell. It was a handy little place, stocking everything of the cheaper variety, and Maggie earned a frugal living from the coppers which her customers were able to spend. In the small window were open boxes of sweets. Clutching our halfpennies or even, at times, pennies, we would gaze in at all the mouthwatering goodies – lucky tatties (candy covered in sweet cinnamon and sometimes with a halfpenny in the middle, wrapped in greaseproof paper), sherbet fountains, lucky bags, coconut pieces thinly sliced and coated in pink and white sugar, liquorice strips, ogo pogo eyes, Highland toffee, conversation lozenges, macaroon bars – in fact, all things dear to the hearts of children.

Maggie never used a paper bag to dispense sweets. Instead, she would take a page from an old magazine and wind it around her hand to make a cone, the bottom of which she twisted tightly to keep the contents in. This ingenious piece of economy once landed me in trouble with my grandmother. One Sunday, after Sunday School in the church hall, I ran across to Maggie's shop clutching my copy of 'Morning Rays' magazine. When, later, my granny asked what had happened to the magazine I had to admit that I had given it to Maggie to make her paper 'bags'!

Maggie and her sister knew every bairn in the street, and we were always treated with kindness, but no-one was ever given anything 'on tick'. The sisters were adamant in that, and good relations with them always prevailed.

Further up the street was another small shop – again a converted room, and owned by a Mrs Jack, who scraped a living from selling home-made candy and toffee. She also sold 'Oh Baby' chewing gum, but I wasn't allowed to buy that! Jock Wood, below our house, sold all kinds of alcoholic drinks, some straight out of barrels. It was quite a large shop, presided over daily by Jock and his wife, and it had a back room in its dark recesses.

Beyond Links Street, a wider world beckoned. Along the Tarrie was a variety of shops, all more or less next door to each other – Buchan's paper shop-cum-post office, Fred Boyne the barber, a butcher, and a general store, among others, but the largest shop belonged to Jimmy Grant the baker. His premises took up the whole corner of St Clement Street and Lime Street, and Jimmy and his family lived in a house at the back of the shop. They had a nice back green and a high wooden gate opening on to Lime Street. Jim Grant, with his assistant Charlie Wilson from Links Street, was a good baker, and was the only man in the district to own a car - a small Morris with, I think, a dicky seat (a contrivance like a car boot which opened to form a seat for two people). How grand Mr and Mrs Grant and their daughters Madge and Catherine looked when they went for a drive on a Sunday.

Everything sold in the shop was freshly made in the bakehouse further along St Clement Street near the school, and was brought by the bakery lad in the traditional manner, on a large tray balanced on his head. Grant's (or, in our vernacular, 'Gruntie's') scones, cream buns, cakes, dough rings, doughnuts and other fancies sold at 2d. for five or 3d. for seven – not dear, but still out of reach for those in really impoverished circumstances. Such people lived on scrape-on-scrape-off bread and margarine, if they were lucky.

For a penny each Grant's sold delectable mince pies, and if a plate was brought the pies would be served hot with gravy, still for only a penny. Pennies were somewhat scarce for us, but we usually managed a pie on a Saturday before going to the weekly matinee at the 'Starrie', the fondly-remembered Star Picture Palace in Park Street. By 'we' I mean myself,

Andrew and Georgie – they had to take me everywhere, and what a nuisance I, who had yet to reach school age, must have been to them.

Next to Buchan the newsagent was a small general store owned by a Mr Allen, a rather grumpy fellow who never smiled, and who, unlike Maggie Caie, never allowed children any time to pick and choose sweets. He obtained his custom mainly through keeping his shop open later than others, Saturdays and Sundays included. He was known as 'The Ha'penny Miser', which was a little paradoxical as he absolutely detested being given halfpennies when a purchase was made. I remember being sent one day for three cream snowballs costing a halfpenny each, and with three of the hated coins in my hand I was, to say the least of it, apprehensive – in fact, feart! Mumbling and complaining, he took the money and grudgingly threw the bag of snowballs on to the counter. I fled. A strange man indeed, who, in making his meagre living in his nice clean shop, harboured such a dislike of the humble maik!

Fred Boyne's was one of the two barber's shops in our area. Not only did Mr Boyne attend to the hairdressing needs of the men of Fittie and St Clements, but he also kept a section of his shop entirely as a ladies salon. Middle-aged and older women in those days usually grew their hair long and tied it into a simple bun at the back, but younger women had quite a variety of styles to choose from. A young lady hairdresser was employed to cut and to bob, and to put in Marcel waves. This was before the days of the permanent wave, and Marcel waving was an alternative to the Eton Crop (a very short, straight, masculine style, favoured by young 'flappers' daring enough to try it). Considerable skill was required with large metal tongs which, after being heated over a gas ring, were used to push and shape the hair into tight, regular waves. By the standards of today its corrugations looked impossibly stiff, but at the time it was considered lovely and glamorous, just like the film stars who made it popular.

'The Deifer', whose name I never knew, was the area's other barber. He worked in a shop on Miller Street, near Church Street, an area with several shops including a chemist. He was a youngish man with dark, sleeked hair and a pale complexion, and he was stone deaf. He could, however, lip-read so well that he had no trouble in communicating with customers, to whom he spoke just a few words in the very soft tone that is peculiar to certain people with defective hearing. My father, after a trip to sea, loved to sit in the barber's chair for a haircut and shave. As a little girl, I would sometimes go with him just to watch. My father had slightly protruding ears, and I remember how 'The Deifer', while snipping away with the scissors, would look at me smilingly, hold my father's ear and pretend to snip it. My father laughed too, and by that I knew that the man was only joking.

Children also came to his shop to have their hair cut. Usually the girls had it semi-shingled at the back, an effect achieved through ruthless use of

Not quite a Marcel wave, but a later, more elaborate version.

Many St. Clements folk would have been very glad to be able to buy Co-op tea in 1932!

the hand clippers. All girls wore their hair in a fringe at the front. When the bob came into fashion, I rebelled at being told to have the old semi-shingle. Off I went to 'The Deifer', looked at him and silently mouthed 'A bob, please'. He looked back at me, shook his head and said in his soft, halting way 'No, your ma said semi-shingle'. I again emphasised 'A bob!', and this time he gave in. Certainly his nickname was a cruel one, but it was a hard world. He was a friendly man, an excellent barber, and much liked by the community.

Across the road from St Clement Street School were the shops of the Northern Co-operative Society, and above these were flats known as the 'Copie houses'. The shops comprised a baker, a butcher and a grocery, the latter having a 'buttery' counter with a wide marble shelf at the back, on to which was deposited 'lump butter' from barrels. Pairs of wooden pats were used to manipulate the butter, a quarter pound at a time, into nice oblong shapes with ridged patterns on them, and the man who did this was a real expert. Also sold from this counter were bacon, cheese, cold meats and dairy products – not pre-packaged as they usually are today, but measured out loose. Under the shelves on the grocery side was a series of built-in bins with sloping sides for easy access. These contained sugar, rice and all manner of other dry goods. The assistants (all male) were fast and efficient, and in any spare minute could be seen weighing and packaging goods in pounds and half pounds – best sugar in blue bags, the ordinary in white. Syrup (nice and cheap) was sold loose, poured from a tap into glass jars which we brought. Many a jar we had of what we chauvinistically referred to as 'Torry jam'!

I would be sent to the Co-op baker by my grandmother for a 'new' or a 'cutting' loaf – both plain white and costing about 4d. each. They came wrapped in light brown tissue paper which we did not discard – it came in very useful for polishing our windows later. A 'cutting' loaf was for immediate use; a 'new' loaf was still warm and steaming from the baker's oven, and would be kept for later in the week. In return for running this little errand I would be rewarded with the warm heel of the new loaf, deliciously spread with syrup. Other favourites besides the excellent bread and rowies were baps covered in fine white flour, and Vienna rolls – square in shape with a raised, crusty top and a softer part underneath. These were a treat at breakfast time, especially with jam or marmalade inside. Everything was absolutely fresh from the bakehouse every morning at six o'clock. If, however, my father's trip at sea was longer than usual, we had to do without such luxuries and be content simply with toast or with porridge and a spoonful of condensed milk on top!

Everything at the Co-op had to be paid for over the counter (no 'tick'), and on quoting a personal number the customer was given a reclaimable dividend cheque. Customers would rattle off their numbers with ease, and

I can still remember those of my aunt, my mother and my grandmother. The twice-yearly 'divi' was generous at 3s. 7d. in the pound, and was relied upon by many to make up rent payments, which were also due every six months, but Co-op divis did not give much help to the large number of people in St Clements who had great difficulty in finding as much as a pound to spend. The Co-op shops, which were the only really large ones in the area, tended to sell goods in greater bulk than many prospective customers could afford, and so numerous small 'Johnny A'thing' shops like Maggie Caie's thrived. They were convenient, remaining open after the Co-op had closed, and were able to supply small amounts of sugar, tea, etc when these ran out.

On the corner of Miller Street and Baltic Street was Jones' provisions shop, known as the 'Baggie Shop' or 'Baggie Jones' after the twopenny bags of biscuits and sweets that were sold there. I would not care to vouch for the freshness of the biscuits, but those 'baggies' were very popular. Strathdee's Bakery, between Jim Grant's and St Clement Street School, was particularly well patronised on Tuesdays at about midday when a small crowd would gather at the door awaiting the arrival of a van bringing large bags of yesterday's buns, cakes and teabread. The bags were not particularly cheap at 3d., but they were full of goodies which, if not absolutely fresh, were still very tasty. A neighbour, Mrs Walker at No. 6 Links Street, maintained that from one threepenny bag she could get a 'fancy piece' for her fly-cup as well as having plenty left to make a dumpling!

Jam jars and soft drink bottles could be cashed in to obtain a halfpenny worth of soft brown sugar from Banks' dry goods store on the corner of Baltic Street. The sugar was served in a grey cone-shaped bag and was ideal for eating by the finger-licking method.

There were many more shops in the 'square' at the top of the Tarrie, including A.B. Hutchison's bakery, a shoemaker, a general goods shop and a newsagent. Across the 'square' was the chemist (Wattie Bain) and near the corner of Garvock Street a general merchant who made and sold excellent 'potted heid' at a penny a small bowl. This shop also vied with Hunter's in Church Street in the sale of fruit and vegetables.

It is worth mentioning that nobody that I knew of owned a chip-pan. For one thing, a large quantity of fat would have had to be purchased, so instead Mr Davidson's chip shop next to the school did a steady trade. His fish and chips were excellent, and he was usually at his busiest on Friday and Saturday nights. There were also chip shops in Garvock Street and, I think, Wellington Street.

Luxuries were few and far between, and under this heading came many domestic products that are taken more or less for granted nowadays. No tablet of scented toilet soap would, for instance, be found on the average person's sink. Instead, a piece of ordinary coarse household soap served

27

alike for washing dishes, scrubbing the floor and washing hands. Newspapers cut into squares and hung on a nail in the 'water closet', as my grandmother so loftily called the lavatory, were the 'soft toilet tissue' of the time. Generally speaking, the food which we ate in those days was plain and simple, bought on a daily basis while there were a few coppers left. Soup made with boiled bones was very popular, especially if the butcher was generous and gave the bones free of charge. Vegetables were organically grown, using only farm manure as fertiliser, and eggs called to mind a picture of their being laid in the straw by some happy hen which spent its days clucking around the farmyard, like hens should. One thing that my Grandfather very much enjoyed was a duck (he always called it 'dyuck') egg for his 6 o'clock supper. In one of our various little family rituals, he would take his knife, carefully cut the top from the egg, and offer the piece (which he did not like!) to me for dutiful acceptance.

My mother liked to shop at the market in the Green (the 'Greenie Market') for country produce, including, if funds allowed, lovely fresh 'newly laid' eggs. 'Vegetables taste better from the Greenie', she declared, and I have no doubt that they did. Not surprisingly, fish became at times almost our staple diet. At the end of a trip to sea, trawlermen always, as I have mentioned, received a large bass bag full of fish. There were no fridges in those days, so some of the fish was given to neighbours. Later the bass bags of other trawlermen in the street would be shared out, and so it went on. Fish cooked in all manner of ways – fried, baked, soup, fish cakes, etc – made a good healthy replacement for butcher meat, which was a scarce commodity on the table. When money was available, we bought Robertson's jam, and through saving the coupons from the jars my mother obtained for me a pretty little enamel golliwog brooch, which I very much treasured.

The day of the television advertisement was still a long way off, and brightly coloured posters on hoardings were used extensively for the promotion of cigarettes, soaps and foods of all kinds. The Bisto Kids were already long-established favourites, the little boy and girl urchins sniffing the delicious aroma of this brand of gravy – 'Ahh, Bisto!'

My grandfather's daily walk to and from work took him along the Quays, across Regent Bridge and past the Fish Market, where every now and then he would purchase two large partans (crabs). These would be tied up in a cotton net cloth and brought home alive. My Grandmother would at once put the big black boiling pot full of water on the hob. When the water was boiling, she would drop in the partans and put on the lid. I didn't like that bit at all, but I did enjoy my share of the crab meat, picked out with a hairpin.

Occasionally we would have prawns, still in their shells and boiled in the big pot. These were a real delicacy. Often our other foods were accompanied by skirlie; stovies were good too, and cheap, so we had lots of them. My mother, who was a very good and imaginative cook, made excellent steak pies, funds permitting, and we would sometimes have some kind of rice or milk pudding on a Sunday, but not at any other time – the 42 shillings a week that my father received was no great fortune when a growing family such as ours had to be clothed and fed.

Money was scarce for everyone. A pound of mince at 4d., a loaf of bread 3d. or 4d., bacon a luxury at 8d. per pound – those prices sound so tiny nowadays, but the average working man's wage, let alone the pittance which passed for Broo or Parish benefits, made little provision for eating wholesomely and well. I recall one Links Street family's little ones coming careering down their tenement stairs one Sunday morning proclaiming to everyone 'We got a half egg each for oor breakfast'! Any windfalls were therefore very welcome. When, for instance, a large glut of potatoes occurred late one summer, word went round that surplus stocks were to be handed out free from Seggie's goods shed on the Links close by Wellington Street. The shed was a large wooden structure, filled on this occasion with potatoes by the ton. Everyone descended on the great give-away with buckets, pails, bags, etc, which we children filled by means of shovels. A most extraordinary occurrence.

Then one dark wintry night in January 1929 there was the grounding, on Aberdeen beach near the Bathing Station, of the steamer *Idaho*. At the first blare of her siren, most of the people of Fittie and St Clements were down on the sands armed with tin baths, bags, buckets, basins and barrows, for they knew that there would be coal.

The water was calm and shallow, and the ship and its crew were quite safe. The vessel would have to be lightened in order that an attempt might be made to refloat her at the next high tide, and it seemed certain that her coal bunkers would be unloaded into the water. We were not disappointed. I was left to guard our three-wheeled barrow (made by my grandfather, as were so many of our wooden artefacts) while holding aloft a storm lantern. The rest of the family waded in for the coal, along with all other adults who were fit and able. I stood by with some other children, watching over our share as it came up from the ship. The *Idaho* was in fact to remain stuck on the sands for months – it was not until August that she was at last floated off and taken to the harbour. She finally went to the breakers. Meanwhile, our coal cellars were full 'to the gunwales', as Granda would say, and we had fine fires in our grates that winter.

Our coal cellars were situated beneath the tenement, and were approached from the lobby via a back door which opened on to our postage stamp-sized backie. Outside, on the left was Beldie's kitchen window, in front were two water closets and to the right the wash house. A steep flight of stone stairs led to 'the sunks' – a dark, damp dungeon-like area with a cobbled floor and with coal cellars ranged around it. I had sometimes to accompany Georgie when he went to fetch a pailful of coal, my job being to take charge of the illumination – a candle in a saucer-shaped candleholder. I didn't care for that. The place was so eerie, and Georgie's reassurance 'Never mind, there's nae ghosties' was of no help!

Back to the Tarrie. 'What you've never had you'll never miss' was a common saying in those days. We never had a bathroom or a fitted toilet, and we never knew anyone else who had. Some tenements were far better than others – Torry, for instance, had good solid granite ones, especially in Victoria Road, but even these were devoid of bathrooms or hot running water. Very few tenement flats had electricity; those that did usually had a small geyser which gave hot water at the sink. In most houses gas-light was the only illumination, so old Maggie Caie did a good trade in the antiquated and infuriatingly frail gas mantle.

Most of the houses on the Tarrie were ranged along one side from the school to the corner of Wellington Street. They were tenements, as in Links Street, but were of better quality. Their lobbies and stairs were floored with brown ship's linoleum, and each stair had a metal strip along the edge to prevent wear. Best of all, though, they had toilets off each landing, and very posh some of these were, with even a brass pull chain. Some of the landing windows contained little coloured glass squares, which shut out any harsh light and lent an air of privacy to the house. The tenants there were fortunate – no going out to back-yard 'lavvies' in all kinds of weather for them, although doubtless they paid handsomely for such amenities. The 'Copie' houses were also quite impressive, no doubt with indoor water closets and with stained glass in their stairway windows as well. I never saw inside one, as we would very quickly have been chased out if we had ventured into any of those stairways!

In a ground-floor flat at No. 30 St Clement Street lived my great-aunt, Mary Jane Smith. The building stood on the corner of Lime Street and had a side gate similar to Jim Grant's opposite. At the back was a nice drying green with coal cellars and wash houses around it. The flats were of three rooms instead of the usual two, and there were toilets off the entrance lobby and stair landings. No gas jets here – this tenement had electricity even in the lobby, where a lantern-style shade on the ceiling light gave an air of grandness with its subdued colours. The lobby was floored with small terra-cotta tiles set in a pattern.

I can never think of Fittie's St Clements area and my childhood there without remembering with fondness Mary Jane and her family. Widowed when the youngest of her seven children, Phyllis, was eight or nine years old (there were 22 years between Phyllis and her eldest child, Nan), she was given invaluable support by the older members of the family, four of whom lived in America. Letters from New York invariably contained some dollars, so that no hardship was suffered by their beloved mother, and when two of the remaining family, Ethel and Bert, both left to be married, one daughter, Ina, came home from the States. I loved to go into the Smiths' cosy kitchen, similar in style to my grandmother's but fitted with a tiled grate and small cooker above it. The sink top was tiled as well, and the table, which sat in the centre of the room, was kept covered with a cloth. Two shelves of the front room cupboard or 'press' were always laden with a wide range of real home-made fruit jams and jellies. Mary Jane always referred to jam as 'berries', and to be asked what kind of 'berries' I wanted on my softie was a great treat. Every Easter, Mary Jane gave to me, my sister and my brothers (when they came on the scene) each a hard-boiled egg, dyed different colours and duly admired before being taken to the Broad Hill for rolling. Sunday tea-time treat at this family's table was a plate of 'fancy pieces' from the Co-op. Mary Jane liked Co-op baking best, especially a type of sponge cake wrapped around with greaseproof paper and known as a 'sair heidie'!

In the Smiths' front room was a fine old piano – a German overstrung instrument with a beautifully polished dark wood case and an ornate front on which was a pair of candle-holders which swivelled back when not in use. I loved to play it and to listen to its rich tone. By this time I was at school, where an instruction class in piano or violin was on offer, and I so badly wanted to have piano lessons. I almost drove my mother to distraction with my pleas, but she simply could not afford 12s. 6d. per quarter at a time when the size of our family was increasing and every penny had to be counted.

It could at times be almost an escape to visit the Smiths, not just because of the piano or the treats, but because of the household's jolly, charismatic atmosphere. Mary Jane was never severe; she always wore a smile, and the house was pervaded by a feeling of comfort, well-being and family affection. The house had, of course, no bathroom, but a basin filled with hot water would be put in front of a cheery fire for the girls to wash in before they sat down at the breakfast table. Their mother would fuss over them with tea, morning rowies, softies, Vienna rolls and of course her home made 'berries'.

The Smiths' American connections made them unique in the community, and during the Depression years I would pester Ina for stories about New York and the people that had been reduced to hoboes and vagrants by the terrible effects of the slump. Also through the Smiths I was introduced to American comics, which were sent to Phyllis at regular intervals. They were quite different from ours, and although I enjoyed the usual 'Sunbeam',

'Funny Wonder' and 'Comic Cuts', there was a fascination about characters like Little Orphan Annie and Li'l Abner.

In 1929, Phyllis and her mother were treated by the family to a holiday in America. How envious I felt as I watched them leave in a taxi, their cabin trunk and other luggage strapped to the back of the car. Imagine an ordinary Aberdeen working class family sailing to New York at a time when for most people a trip to Cults on the 'subbie' was enough to make a red letter day! On her return, Phyllis was surrounded by the kids of our street as she regaled them with her best American accent. She also brought home some lovely dresses, one of which, a pink georgette, I was allowed to borrow for the Sunday School Christmas party that year.

On one or two occasions, Phyllis, the larky school-girl, accompanied me to the Starrie's Saturday matinee. She objected to sitting downstairs in the stalls, so up to the balcony we had to go – and it cost 3d. each for the privilege. Once we bought from the sweet shop in Wales Street a supply of monkey-nuts in their shells; Phyllis took two of these nuts, made a small split in the top of each shell, and fixed them to her ear-lobes as 'long earrings'. In that way we were able to ingeniously (and cheaply) deck ourselves just like the glamorous female star on the screen! Another time, Ethel Smith and her fiancé took me to His Majesty's Theatre. They had bought a ticket for Mary Jane, but she did not wish to go, so I went instead to see the play 'Mother Of Pearl' – my first-ever theatre visit.

Mary Jane's family had one other distinction in the community – one of her sons had been goal-keeper for Aberdeen Football Club. Mary Jane had a ticket for the Pittodrie stand, from where she watched him with pride. Anyone shouting anything uncomplimentary would find themselves in receipt of rather more than they had bargained for!

From the time of my fifth birthday onwards, I found my mode of life changing. I now had a sister, next my brother James was born, and at about the time of James's arrival I took a major step in the world...

CHAPTER 3
WORK AND PLAY

For any child, the first day at school is a big event. In my case it was eagerly anticipated, Georgie having assured me that *he* liked school, and that I would be given a reading book and a schoolbag to keep it in. I had therefore few qualms as I put on my smart new navy blue serge dress with pleats, my navy blue socks and my black patent leather shoes. My hair had been neatly trimmed, and a studio photograph taken of me in this attire, standing by a table with a vase of flowers on it. My school was of course St Clement Street School close by, and with my Granny's entreaty to 'be a good quinie' I walked across the playground with my mother on that first morning, entering through the door that had the words 'Mixed Infants' engraved on the stone above it.

Clutching my mother's hand, I went into the classroom to find a harassed teacher trying to cope with a class of tearful children and their worried mothers. One little girl called Julia was so determined to go home again that, howling, she gave the teacher a kick. The teacher, Miss Jamieson, calmed her down and gave her a piece of Fry's cream chocolate. Later I complained to my mother and granny 'It wisna fair – I was quiet and didna kick the teacher, but Julia did and got some chocolate!'

Miss Jamieson, a middle-aged lady, wore a black cross-over overall with long sleeves and kept her greying wispy hair tied in a bun at the back. Kindly and patiently, she taught us our first letters and numbers as we sat at the desks with their varnished lids and attached wooden seats. For writing exercises we did not use pen and paper – instead we used slate pencils, always keeping pieces of rag to wipe the slates clean. This was usually done by the 'spit-and-rub' method, but the slates, which were fixed in narrow but strong wooden frames, stood up to the punishment. They belonged to the school, but we had to provide our own slate pencils; I bought mine from Maggie Caie.

In a corner of the classroom was an old-fashioned piano, which Miss Jamieson would sometimes play for us; we learned to sing a little song, 'High Up In The Oak Tree Lived An Elf', and one day we were asked if any of us could play. My granny being one of the fortunate few who had a piano, I put up my hand. The class was then treated to a one-finger version of 'Bells Of The Sea'!

At playtime, we would take our 'pieces' and eat them in the playground, Miss Jamieson feeding the sparrows with any crumbs that were left. At the sound of the handbell, we would line up to troop back inside, some of the older pupils singing 'Come in an' get kilt, Come in an' get kilt' to the bell's rhythm and also to the considerable annoyance of the bell ringer, usually a teacher named Miss Taylor. Soon we had our Chambers' first reading book and were learning all about how 'The man at the hut had ten hens, A dog and a cat; The dog sat on the rug, The cat sat on the mat.' I was given a school satchel, just as Georgie had described, and in it my very first, very special school book was taken home. My mother carefully fitted the book with a cover made from a piece of last year's slightly faded kitchen table oil-cloth (nothing was wasted). The turned-in edges were sewn from top to bottom. Next she crocheted a woollen chain with a small disc as bookmark and thumb rest – very ingenious, and the pages were kept clean. Reading, as soon as I had mastered it, became my favourite pastime, though Granny, who would have much preferred me to learn to knit and do something with my hands, called it an idle one!

The girls, when a little older, had a weekly sewing and knitting class with a Miss Brydon. From our own lengths of cotton cloth (costing only a few coppers) we made 'lap bags'. These were like aprons with a folded-up flap in front, deep enough to hold all our 'work', as the teacher called it. We had to embroider the edges in simple basic stitches, then embroider our initials on the front, in the centre. This took several weeks, and a neat job was rewarded with a single strand of coloured silk embroidery thread, drawn from a skein and carefully placed on the recipient's shoulder. Not being exactly the crème de la crème of this class, I cannot remember ever having been given one of these coveted threads! The lap bags completed, we went on to make cotton frocks. These were very basic, rather awful-looking garments, resembling bags with short sleeves, but they were still preferable to what followed – matching bloomers! Some of our clumsy efforts must have tried the patience even of good teachers like Miss Brydon, but through perseverance (on her part as well as our own) we learned to hand-sew. For knitting lessons we were issued with pairs of short steel knitting needles and small balls of wool. At the teacher's desk there waited a perpetual queue for help with dropped stitches, and some pupils finished up with more than the original number of cast-on stitches on their needles, but we learned this domestic art as was expected of us – for after all wasn't it woman's work?

Diversions were always welcome during classroom hours, and we particularly enjoyed the annual invasion of our school by students collecting money for charity during Rag Week. Clowns, young men in gym slips and long artificial pleated hair, babies with dummies, they would bounce into our classroom, and we would readily part with our halfpenny or penny as the tins were rattled at us.

On one occasion, our class made its way 'crocodile-style' to the old prom, where we waved little Union Jacks as Edward, Prince Of Wales, passed by in his car. He smiled and waved to us as the car made its way at a brisk pace towards Wellington Street, no doubt on its way to the Town

House. Later, Edward became King Edward VIII but was never crowned. He abdicated after only 325 days, on 10 December 1936, because of his determination to marry the American divorcée Mrs Wallis Simpson. 'No Morganatic Marriage', announced the newspaper headlines; we had a new King and Queen, George VI and Elizabeth. Stories and films seem to suggest that in Edward Britain would have had a playboy King – but we had no idea of such things on that sunny day on the prom.

With childhood diseases rife, there were always absences from school for one reason or another, but any family whose child was absent for more than four days would be visited by a representative of the education authority – the 'Tak'-A'', whose job it was to make sure that the reason for absence was a genuine one, and to report back to the school. 'Tak'-A' wore a navy blue uniform and a hard-top cheesecutter cap, marks of officialdom which occasioned respect. Paltry excuses such as 'I had to keep her off school to watch the bairn on washing-day' did not impress him; if we wanted a day off we had to be very convincingly 'ill', otherwise we would be told 'The Tak'-A' will come looking for you!' It was seldom worth the trouble.

Some of the notes sent to teachers by parents explaining the absence of their children must have occasioned great amusement – I remember hearing of one that read:

'Dear Teacher,

Please excuse —— for being absent, as she had the boil.'

Of course it meant 'the bile', but we were taught to speak what was referred to as 'plain English' from our earliest schooldays, and notes such as this were not uncommon!

My first headmaster was a Mr Ogilvie, a very tall, grey-haired, smartly-dressed, genial man. He would never enter a classroom without first tapping on the upper, plain glass part of the door with a pencil or pen. The glass had a frosted pattern for three quarters of its height, but Mr Ogilvie was so tall that we could all see him before he tapped and walked briskly in. Before he retired to Edinburgh he asked my grandfather to build him a model of a lifeboat on which some of his former pupils from old Fittie village had served. He was so proud of these brave lads that when he left Aberdeen he took with him a beautiful miniature wooden replica of their boat, complete with oars, but made from no plan or blue-print, only memory and a love of ships.

After the freedom of our first long summer holidays, the prospect loomed of the impending return to school. Once again Miss Jamieson's infant class would be filled, while for the older pupils to whom she had taught the rudiments of literacy and numeracy, education would begin in earnest. To enforce discipline, a tawse or belt was kept in each teacher's desk. Even Miss Jamieson had one, so soft that it would not hurt a fly. 'A pandy, a pandy, a smack on the handie', we chanted, but things were different from our second year onwards. Discipline in the more senior classes was strict, and misdemeanours were punished by 'pandies' of the kind that left red weals on the skin.

In March 1930 there arrived from Ferryhill School a new headmaster, Mr Martin, who tested classes for handwriting and in such subjects as mental arithmetic, which I detested. Anyone yawning or fidgeting was liable to find a piece of chalk heading his or her way at great speed. Plenty of homework was given, and any neglect of it was answered with the belt. Somehow, though, the homework was done, and school became interesting. Multiplication tables were learned parrot-fashion, a method which seemed to work well, and were not easily forgotten. To the teacher's great relief, tables such as those of measurement were chanted easily.

Cleverer pupils sat in the back row of the classroom, towards which the floor slanted upwards, the rows of desks divided by a central passageway. The rest of the thirty or so children were ranged according to their ability so that the less apt sat in the front seats under the teacher's eye. No chewing of gum was allowed; anyone found doing so would be publicly made to deposit the offending material in the waste paper basket.

The school day began at 9 a.m. with assembly in the main hall. After that, to a march played on the piano by one of the teachers, we trooped to our classrooms. Laughter and scuffles followed until the teacher arrived to curb our youthful exhuberance. Miss Gillespie, on the mornings when she took our first lesson, would sweep in, clap her hands and exclaim 'Empty barrels make the most noise!' Class teachers had to cover all of the 'three R's', Geography, History, etc – in fact, everything except Music and P.T.

On bitterly cold winter mornings when snow and icicles hung from the roofs (a common sight in those days), we would gladly enter the centrally-heated classroom and warm our hands and feet on the clinking, clanking pipes and radiators. This luxury was short lived. The teacher would enter the room, sniff disdainfully and open the windows, pulling them down at the top with a long pole. In her defence, it must be said that the air was often rather fetid due to the unwashed state of the clothes of pupils who lived in overcrowded, unhygienic conditions.

Those who had brought a playtime 'piece' – perhaps toast or a rowie wrapped in a bag – were allowed to put it on the pipes to heat, and when the teacher relented and closed the windows again the air became filled with the delicious aroma of the buttery roll. At the interval bell the lucky owners of the 'pieces' would retrieve them, and those who had a halfpenny could buy a ⅓ pint bottle of milk and a straw. I usually received a halfpenny for this purpose, although with three of our family at school, milk money was not guaranteed.

36

The new school session meant new school books, and for these, as my father was employed, I brought home a bill for 6s. – a whole day's wages for a trawlerman. Books had to be handed down through families, and so were kept clean and neat. Anyone who could not afford to buy books was given worn, used ones from the teacher's cupboard. Such frugal living was accepted as normal in St Clements, just as it was in so many other places, and yet, when the big wall map of the world was unrolled for Geography lessons, so many areas were seen to be coloured pink. Great Britain governed all of these, filling its coffers from every corner of the globe. It seemed inconceivable that amid all these riches people were living in the abject poverty of the workless, or were working long hours for the poorest of wages, with no support in case of industrial accident or any other mishap which could put the victim among the ranks of the unemployed. At St Clement Street School we learned all about pounds, shillings and pence from our highly professional, well-educated, middle-class teachers. We knew that there were 12 pennies in a shilling, and 20 shillings and 240 pennies in a pound, but we also knew that a pound was a lot of money, and not easily come by.

Adding a column in the old coinage was awkward as there were so many different values. Of course we called them by their nicknames – a bob, a tanner, half-a-crown, a florin, and so on, but we were never allowed to refer to them as such. We were not permitted to speak in the Doric, and I think this stifled what we had to say and made us less articulate.

Now and then the class would be taken by a student teacher, and one day we had in our midst a very handsome young man who was immediately appraised by the girls as 'a richt sheik'. Our regular teacher not being present (she was probably in the staff room marking homework) the unfortunate young fellow was ribbed unmercifully. The boys fired paper pellets from their rulers, but it was the girls in the front seats (older than the rest of us and 'kept back' from the previous year) who caused us the most amusement. Each time the student turned, chalk in hand, to write on the wall blackboard, a chorus of chirping or wolf-whistles went up from these girls, causing him to blush furiously, but even his authority finally prevailed. He taught us spelling and dictation, and there was a whole penny for the pupil who could spell 'rheumatism' correctly. I won the penny for giving the closest answer – student teachers were fun!

Once a week we went for P.T. (then known as 'drill') in the main hall. The teacher was a mature lady in a short gym slip, navy blue knickers, white blouse and long black cashmere stockings. Most gym knickers had a small patch pocket in the front of them, and we had great fits of giggles when, one day when she had a cold, the teacher kept lifting the front of her gym slip, pulling a little handkerchief from the pocket, blowing her nose, then carefully replacing the hanky. I do not think she ever realised what was making us laugh.

Sports Day practice meant a trip to the Links for races, high-jumping and other games. The cream of that day's athletes were chosen as competitors for the big occasion. My best was the high jump, but athlete I was not, and I never achieved much distinction in that respect. These little outings did, neverthless, make a pleasant change from the daily round of lessons.

Our school playground was, like most, segregated by a metal railing into boys' and girls' sides. This left the boys in peace to play marbles ('bools') and rougher games like leap-frog, to stand in groups smoking cinnamon sticks, or to exchange cigarette cards. The girls played 'Tig' or 'One Two Buckle My Shoe' with skipping ropes when these games were in season. Occasionally, quarrels led to fisticuffs, most often among the girls and brought on by envy, perhaps at the parading of, say, a new pair of white 'jimmies'. The challenge 'Fit are you lookin' at?' would be rejoindered with something like 'I dinna ken, it hisna got a number', and blows would ensue between starer and stared-at. Once I had a tussle with a girl named Winnie Coombs from William's Square, off Garvock Wynd, that very crowded corner of St Clements, containing much very poor housing. Winnie and I were in fact very close friends during school hours, but that did not stop us. Sheer youthful exuberance, I suspect.

Our history lessons were mainly about English monarchs and were dry as dust, although we did remember what we were told about the Highland Clearances, Culloden, Bannockburn, the Jacobite Rebellion, etc. We were taught nothing about the recent Great War, and could of course have had no inkling that our age group would one day be involved in another international conflict. In music class we learned songs, mainly Scottish ones which we sang with great gusto – 'Charlie Is My Darling', 'Johnny Cope', 'Will Ye No' Come Back Again'. We read out 'Lorna Doone', 'Kidnapped' and works by Dickens in class, the teacher becoming so exasperated with slow, halting readers that she delegated the task to the more learned among us, which was much less hard on her nerves. Poetry was chanted ('Men must work, Women must weep, And the harbour bar be moaning'), and we were taught Shakespeare and, of course, Burns, but poetry was not much appreciated. Arithmetic was not our favourite subject either, but gradually we got through the fractions and decimals. Through the patience of a kind elderly teacher, Mr Young, our learning of long division felt like pieces of a jigsaw falling into place.

Headmaster Mr Martin stood no nonsense from anyone, and his visits to take over our class (especially for mental arithmetic sessions) caused us some anxiety. One day he gave us a handwriting test, dictating a passage while the class wrote. I decided to employ a little strategy. Our own teacher, Mr Paterson, was patrolling the desks; when he saw my handwriting he gave me a hard nudge on the shoulder and whispered

'You great goat!' But I knew that Mr Martin liked large rounded lettering, and I was out to please him. The ruse worked, and much to Mr Paterson's amazement and chagrin I received Mr Martin's warm approval!

Some pupils, unfortunately, never did make much academic progress despite all the efforts of their teachers, whose exasperation led on occasion to extreme use of the dreaded belt (although I never saw Mr Young do this). These children were 'kept back', never to reach the eleven-plus or 'qually' class which would have taken them to Frederick Street Intermediate School and the Lower Leaving Certificate. The ambition of most parents was to have their elder offspring leave school at the age of 14, improving the family's finances through finding some kind of employment. There was no Government help, and life could be a terrible struggle for larger families, however strong the pride which permeated their close-knit relationships. Further education was considered to be a leisurely pursuit for the more privileged classes.

One fine sunny June Sunday I was standing in the street with my mother when a large charabanc drew up. The vehicle, which seemed to take up the street's whole width, had two doors and a canvas roof which folded down to reveal soft upholstered seats in the capacious interior. Mothers and children living on the slender means of the Parish were being taken on a picnic, privately provided as a special treat. The prospect was exciting. The picnic was to take place at Bieldside, which for us was a long way off. Some of the smaller children were rather apprehensive about boarding this awesome-looking thing, but were urged on with 'Ye're ga'n tae see coos an' sheep an' hae a rare hurl on the charabanc, so stop greetin'! Their unseen, unknown benefactor would have been happy to see the joy and anticipation that his generosity brought.

I so wanted to go in the charabanc, and stood greeting until my mother gave me a dunt on the shoulder. 'Ye canna ging on the charabanc – yer Da's workin!' That was the end of that. Young as I was, I knew that there were no free treats if your Da was in employment. The charabanc set off amid cheers, waving and much honking of the horn. Boys tried to cling on to the back for a free hurl, but soon gave up as the vehicle turned the corner into St Clement Street. Pearson's Picnic was under way.

Every year, with great panache, the residents of Fittie village held their own picnic. A mass exodus of children and adults, led by Oakbank School Boys Pipe Band, marched proudly along York Street then along the Quays, the crewmen of ships at anchor waving cheerily to them as they passed. The happy crowd thronged the railway station, where, before the train was boarded, chocolate bars were purchased from the big red Nestlé's (pronounced 'Nessles', of course) slot machines. A penny in the slot, a strong pull on the metal drawer, and out came the familiar silver-wrapped, red-banded bar from the rows visible through the machine's front glass. Filled with happy, waving people, the train carrying the Fittie Picnic puffed from the station, bound most years for Milltimber – an expedition to foreign parts in those days when the world was a much larger place.

Our Sunday School picnic was also a great institution. Held usually in August, it was much looked forward to by the members and children of St Clement's Church. One warm sultry day I, my grandmother, Andrew, Georgie, and various other relatives set off on the special train to Drum. In the picnic field, families sat on raincoats and small blankets around the barbed wire fence. Tea was served to the adults and milk to the children, and everyone received a bag of buns and a cake. Dressed in a white frock, with white socks and shoes, I was urged to enter the races which were in progress.

The air became ever more sultry and oppressive, until at last what we most dreaded happened – an electrical storm, the worst that I can remember, with torrential rain, incessant blinding flashes of lightning, and peal after peal of thunder crashing deafeningly over our heads without break. People huddled helplessly around the fence, taking what shelter they could under the trees. Some boys made a sort of tent from small branches covered with their jackets, and from this makeshift shelter in the centre of the field came voices singing 'It ain't gonna rain no mo', no mo', It ain't gonna rain no mo' – such wishful thinking. Sunday School picnics were annual fixtures throughout my childhood, and I relished the thought of a day in the sun, the races and games, and the opportunity to see the farm animals.

A family picnic in the summer made a diversion from the standard routine and environment. Usually in arranging one my mother had some secondary purpose in mind, based on her sense of what was practical, so her favourite spot was the Bay Of Nigg, where we could gather buckies (whelks) while enjoying the fresh air. The Bay was a well-known picnic place, sheltered, with a large flat grassy area in which children could run around safely. A fresh water tap had been set up there too. Off we would go, armed with supplies of potatoes, salt, corned beef and milk, and a cooking pot. On most occasions we travelled to Nigg by bus, which meant some walking at the other end, but we were used to that. The children could not wait to begin gathering dry flotsam and sticks with which we built our little fires amid circles of stones. We would look among the larger rocks for a nice flat one, warmed by the sun, where we could sit in comfort and with a measure of privacy.

We could be quite alone in the little sunlit bay, watching the fishing boats out on the water. In those days it was a beautiful, clean place. When the tide receded, leaving rocky pools, we would set to gathering the buckies from the seaweed-covered rocks and stones to which they clung in dozens.

'If wet, in hall'. A rained off picnic for these St Clement's children in June 1928.

Members of the St. Clement's Church Mothers' Meeting leave the Castlegate for a trip to Alford in July 1928.

All the fun of the fair, even in the midst of the Depression.

The fair in 1935 – now complete with fancy entrance gate!

There were limpets too, but these were inedible and their armour-plating was too efficient for us to be able to chip them off, so we left them alone. Our bare feet comfortable in the warm pools, we turned over stones to uncover little crabs, which scurried away into the soft sand to our squeals of excitement, especially when our toes got too close to them. Meals tasted so much better al fresco, in the open air which made us so hungry.

When the sun began to set at the end of a happy and leisurely day, we would head home with our precious tins and baskets of buckies. The buckies would be thoroughly rinsed and cleaned, then boiled in the big black soup pot. We would have a feast of them, pulling out the meat with hairpins as we sat around the kitchen table, on which was laid a plate for the empty shells and tops.

Berry-picking at 'The Gramps' was also popular with our family. 'The Gramps' were not the Grampian Mountains but the Grampian Hills - the name sometimes given to the Tullos Hill area on which the Kincorth housing estate now stands, and which we would reach by taking a penny-halfpenny 'subbie' train trip to the Bridge Of Dee. Searching among the thick bushes for blaeberries with which to make a pot or two of jam was not the most leisurely of activities, but it still meant a day in the country and a little adventure. But sometimes no money was left for travel, and then we would simply be told 'We're going to Homeallday' or to 'Washallday'!

Each summer, I and my friends spent day after day roaming the beach and Links as far as the Broad Hill. We could do this freely and safely (although we always went in a company of boys as well as girls), and the beach made the best play area that we could have had. Just south of the Beach Ballroom, sheltered by a large grassy knoll, was a bandstand where in summer people sat and listened to army brass bands playing well known tunes. This was very enjoyable and cost nothing, which gave it added appeal as the dole-queues lengthened during the Depression. Aberdeen was at that time a favourite holiday resort, especially with folk from Glasgow who could still afford to go somewhere.

To cater for the crowds, a Pierrot show was put on twice nightly in the bandstand. With a back-drop and stage it made a nice little open-air theatre; folding seats were placed in a railed-off area in front and people were charged a small sum to sit there. We Links Street youngsters came to stand with the throngs outside the railings, usually managing to find our way to the front of the crowd, from where we had an excellent view.

Each show began with a song and dance act by the assembled company – 'Here we are again, Happy as can be, All good friends and jolly good company' – ending with a little flourish of dancing. We enjoyed comedian Gus Strachan and all the other acts with the exception of 'Violet' (Violet Davidson), a lovely soprano who sang songs like 'Doon The Burn, Davie

Lad'. These songs did nothing for us; we had quite enough of that sort of stuff at school! During the show, one of the company would go around the people standing by the fence, shaking a black velvet collection bag with a handle. He shook it in vain under our noses, but did quite well with coppers from the adults. Truly we were all 'Happy as can be'.

Stage-struck from the Pierrot shows, we would invade No. 1 Links Street (the only building in the street with a real drying green) to put on our own backie concerts. These noisy imitations of the Gus Strachan programmes usually ended in our ejection by the irate householders, one of whom, a grim-faced woman by the name of Mrs Vass, of whom we were all feart, would have us taking to our heels through the side gate as soon as we saw her coming!

To the children of Links Street the heralding of summer was the trying out of the first carriage on the beach's huge Scenic Railway, built in 1929. The steep slopes and scary dips of this towering wooden structure (long since vanished) never failed to bring excited screams from the fun-seekers who rode on it. Soon the Carnival or fairground would be reopening after its long winter break, an event which we eagerly awaited.

Of all the amusements at the Carnival, our favourite was the Cake Walk, a sort of narrow tunnel with a heaving floor along which customers tried to walk while holding on to brass rails on either side. The music of the fairground organ blared out all around us as we watched the little roundabouts for the very young, the Chair-O-Planes and the steam boats. The fairground machines were not as sophisticated as those of the present day, but there were many 'live' side-shows such as 'the bearded lady' and other freaks, announced by barkers outside their small marquees. I clearly remember the claim being made that inside one of these tents was a lady only 22 inches tall. Full of scepticism, we went inside to find a young woman dressed in a long white Mae West-style evening dress and high-heeled shoes – and she was, incredibly, only 22 inches tall.

We would watch the holiday-makers as they tried their skill at the win-a-prize stalls, sometimes coming away with a box of sweets or a trinket. Prizes were good, not the plastic stuff that now passes for the name. At that time, people who spent their money on such amusements wanted something worthwhile in return! There was a man who, for a penny, would try to guess one's weight, offering a 'diamond' ring if wrong. Bobby, one of my chums, paid the man to guess my weight. The guess was incorrect, as was proved when I stepped on to the scales. Bobby gave me the ring, saying that we were engaged – we were all of eight years old.

In those long days of sunshine we would run barefoot over the Links to the beach, the swings (which we called the 'showds'), the maypole, the parallel bars, or the 'long logs', huge square wooden beams lying on the grassy area opposite Wellington Street. (These were no doubt cast-offs

Aberdeen's growing popularity as a holiday centre is reflected in this crowded scene of 1929.

Early morning bathing, 1932 style.

from the shipyards – they were there throughout my childhood.) Our first wade in the sea was usually taken in late May, when the sun was warming up but the sea was still cold. Eager anticipation gave our feet increasing momentum over the lush grass with its sprinkling of daisies. With a chorus of Oohs and Aahs, we came upon the hard tarmacadam of the prom, then quickly on to make the first footprints on pristine, newly-washed sands. A sunny morning, with the blue sky reflecting metallically on the sea, the little waves like wisps of lace at the water's edge, ships on the horizon blowing smoke from their funnels, and little fishing boats bobbing about – how lovely it was. As well as the usual sandcastles, we built boats from the wetter sand, forming a hull with our hands. A moat was made around it, and water swirled around our 'boat' as we sat in it.

A favourite game was to hold on to the ropes which slanted down from the salmon nets, holding them upright. As each wave came in, we pulled ourselves up on the ropes to avoid the water. Anyone who did so too slowly got wet! We never waded or swam out of our depth; most of us had learned to swim in the sea at an early age, and we seemed to realise our limitations.

Some of the girls had little brothers and sisters to look after, so we usually had with us a pram or two and some go-cars or push-chairs. A rag-tag-and-bobtail of girls in faded hand-me-down dresses and boys in short trousers and faded shirts, we came equipped with bottles of water and slices of bread spread with margarine and dipped in sugar to ease our hunger pangs until tea time. This was our stretch of beach, the area directly opposite the end of Links Street. We seldom went near the Bathing Station where the holiday folk were, and we never ventured to the Fittie end.

When the beach 'penny baths' did figure in our itinerary, it was usually when the weather was inclement. For our pennies we could have a Saturday morning dip in the fresh, slightly salty, bouyant water which was drawn partly from the sea. It was grand to be able to jump in from the lower diving board, not to mention having such a cheap, easy and pleasurable way of taking a bath! These occasional excursions revealed other delights such as the kiosk which sold spades, pails, beach balls, postcards, water wings, etc, looked at and admired by us but never bought. There was the ice cream stand near the Children's Shelter (for lost children), and music playing over a tannoy system to entertain the crowds. Requests could be made by asking the young man who put on the records.

When we were thirsty there was always a drink of cool fresh water available from one of the wells or water fountains (the 'wallies') spaced at intervals along the prom. Turning a fist-sized knob on one side of these green-painted cast-iron installations produced the drinking water, while turning the knob on the other side produced a cascade of water from a vent at ground level, used for washing sand from the feet.

The beach could be a very busy place, particularly when the holiday crowds from the South came to the city. My mother, who sometimes accompanied us, would exclaim 'My, the beach is jist black wi' folk!' On a warm day, people would dress and undress on the sands, and the sea would be full of people wading, swimming and enjoying the freedom of the seaside, glad to leave their cares behind. Others lolled in deckchairs, eating ice cream as they watched their children play in the sunshine. Everyone was happy in the fine holiday weather and the good clean air, which was so welcomed by those who did not have a beach 'on their doorstep'. We St Clements children were so lucky in having such amenities around us. Indeed, we all had the naïve idea that everybody must have a beach in their town - we simply couldn't imagine anywhere without one.

As a very small girl, I would sometimes be taken to the Carnival by my father as a treat when he came in from sea. After two and sometimes three weeks away I suppose he was making up for lost time! Once he took me on the Scenic Railway, but best of all was the pony rides on the prom, real ponies and carts running up and down a little fenced-in track just next to the cafés. My father, who derived as much pleasure from watching me enjoying myself as from anything, would at length say, 'One mair shottie, then we'll hae a cappie' – another very pleasant thought.

Tired after a day by the sea, we children would occupy the rest of our time in quieter pursuits – bubble-blowing, perhaps. A halfpenny clay pipe from Maggie's, a jam-jarful of soapy water, and bubbles were floating far and wide. An empty lemonade bottle filled with water and a pennyworth of real liquorice stick from Wattie Bain's, and we could make black sugar ale, or 'alie'. The bottle had to be well shaken then put away for a time in a dark place such as a wardrobe. The beverage so produced was well worth the wait.

A visit to the ships berthed at Waterloo Quay or to the lock gate bridge was always of interest. We once watched a diver being readied to enter the green oily water at the lock gates. His heavy, cumbersome attire was topped by a large round helmet with a transparent window. He put on boots with heavy inches-thick metal soles, and lines and tubes were everywhere. We marvelled that he did not sink to the bottom of the harbour straight away. Divers were used to inspect the gates, a job which we did not envy.

Of a summer evening, we would enjoy a stroll along the North Pier, where men and lads could be seen baiting lines and standing patiently awaiting 'a bite'. Fish would be hooked and eagerly pulled in, but often hopes of a tasty supper were dashed when a Fittie voice said, 'It's nae for eatin', loon, it's jist a sadie'. The fish would be thrown back into the water at the sewage outfall area from whence it had come. Further along the pier near the point good fish could be caught with a rod and line, but it was always essential to know clean fish from sadies!

Very warm weather when the sun was strong in the sky (better summers then) brought children on to St Clement Street with the objective of picking at the soft pieces of tarmac that had risen in small bubbles. This was the messiest, stickiest of pastimes, but we all indulged in it at one time or another. My young brother James was enjoying the tar picking one day, when he was given a silver threepenny piece to fetch a message from a nearby shop. When he came to pay for his purchase, the little coin was nowhere to be found. The shopkeeper asked to see both of James' hands. One hand proved to be empty; the other one, which came from behind his back, contained a lump of soft tar, but still no coin. Eventually, after a search, the threepenny was located behind a box of biscuits, where it had fallen from his clean hand!

When a 'tarry biler' arrived, kids would congregate along the pavements to view the fascinating process of road tarring and mending. The men made ready the equipment, which consisted mainly of brushes, pails, and long-handled shovels and spreaders. A fire was lit behind the little metal door under the boiler, which was carried on a metal frame with wheels, and soon the smell of hot tar pervaded the street and houses. Children were encouraged to sniff the fumes in the belief that they were good for the throat and helped to ward off childhood illnesses. We did this willingly as we liked the tarry smell. Pails of hot tar were filled from the boiler, poured over the roadway and spread out evenly with brushes. The tar was then left to glisten on the road until much later when the shovels were used to spread granite chips over it. Finally an enormous steam roller pressed everything down firmly, and once again our Tarrie was smooth and renewed.

Of games we had a rich store – in fact we had so many things to do and so many games to play, especially in summer, that I wonder now how we fitted them all in. In the mornings when the sunlight shone brightly on the opposite side of Links Street, we would go there and play shoppies. Stools, wooden boxes, any old thing was brought on which we could place tin boxes containing little pieces of broken crockery. The more colourful the pieces the better – they represented sweets, and were 'sold' in return for pieces with gold decoration, which were the currency. Papers were brought to wrap the 'purchases' Maggie Caie-style, and while the shoppie craze lasted the discarded sheets made us the bane of the scaffie's life.

Girls spent hours crocheting squares with lengths of left-over wool. Their intention was to join the squares into a blanket, and as each square grew in size it became wonderfully multi-coloured. Every little scrap of wool was begged or borrowed for this industrious occupation, but soon supplies became depleted and enthusiasm waned. The project would then be abandoned until the next year's crocheting 'season'.

Soppy things like shoppies and crocheting were, naturally, not for the boys, but some did participate in skipping, for which we used pieces of back garden washing rope. They showed particular enthusiasm for skipping with double ropes, which we called 'londies'. Bobby and Johnny Mauchline, Teddy Stephen and the Sangster boys, Billy and Stanley, were quite happy to be allowed into this game by the girls.

Very popular was a form of hopscotch called 'Beddies'. A large square was chalked on the pavement then divided into perhaps four smaller squares, each with a number. Each player had a small round piece of wood – a small cairtie wheel with a hole in the centre was ideal. This was cast in a sliding movement on to a numbered square. The player hopped on to the square then with the side of the foot manoeuvred the 'beddie' back to the starting point, moving each foot a square at a time. It was a simple game (if the player did not fall over) and it was also a rather messy one, leaving the pavements thick with chalk! We had kiss-in-the-ring style games – 'The Farmer's In The Dell', 'Little Sally Walker', 'In And Out The Window' - and more boisterous ones like rounders, hide-and-seek, and 'Hoist The Green Flag'. Ball games were also popular, and we sang 'One Two Three A-leary' with its many variations as the ball was dexterously bounced backward and forward.

In summer evenings after shop hours we would play 'hoosies' in the Co-op doorway. The butcher's and the grocery had a shared doorway, nicely paved with small terra-cotta tiles (in the same pattern as was used in some of the tenement houses opposite), and big enough for our games.

Many of our games and pastimes went in 'seasons', and every year the bairns of our area had one for cairties. Some ingenuity was required in the making of a good cairtie, but each consisted basically of a piece of wooden planking, four small wooden wheels, some thickish string and some nails. Pram wheels were much sought after, and anyone who could come by these could make a real limousine. The string was fixed around the wooden front axle so that the cairtie could be steered. Races were held, and many bumps and bruises sustained in the process. When the season ended the cairtie finished up as firewood, usually on Guy Fawkes Night, after being used to wheel around the Guy with the placard around its neck begging for the time-honoured penny. A brand new one would be built the following year.

When our local shops began to sell halfpenny sheets of printed and embossed scraps, quite a craze for these began. A small tin box became a necessity to hold the separated scraps. Some of these were very pretty indeed, with floral designs or (greatly favoured) a little picture of an angel leaning on a fluffy cloud. Through buying and exchanging, we each tried to build up as varied a collection as possible. I joined the Public Library's

Junior Section in Rosemount and in time became an avid reader of Biggles books. I remember one day watching an aeroplane flying high above the church tower. It was a small biplane, similar to those used in the first World War and which we had seen in films when Hollywood portrayed the heroes of that era. People stared up at the sky, watching the aerobatic display as the pilot skilfully put the plane through loops and barrel-rolls. Being well immersed in Biggles stories, I found the sight very appealing. Of course I read other kinds of books as well – I loved 'Little Women', 'Good Wives' and 'Joe's Boys' by Louisa M. Alcott, charming stories of people in another country and a bygone era. Earlier, I had read the fairy tales of Hans Andersen and the Grimms, books which had been given to me as Christmas presents, and all in all I developed a love of reading, although I did tend to choose the 'lighter' material!

Every now and then, a crowd of St Clements children would head for Waterloo Quay where cargo ships unloaded their goods. The quay was usually stacked with timber, while nearby the sheds which took up a whole side of Clarence Street were full of strange commodities. There were bags of cereals and cattle food, the cattle cake (of which there was a manufacturer close by) having a strong, pungent smell. We could find bags of sweet-tasting locust beans – dark brown, vaguely banana-shaped and very good to eat. A torn sack of yellow dried peas would be spotted and pocketfuls appropriated for use in our pea-shooters or 'pluffers'.

Pieces of willowy wood about a yard long would be picked up for a particular use – that of weapons for battle. Thus armed, a crowd of kids from Links Street would line up, confronting another crowd from Clarence Street and Lime Street. The 'enemy' had called our street 'The Jungle', and such words had to be avenged. When the shout of 'Charge' went up, a mob surged on to the Tarrie in front of Strathdee's Bakery to act out a mock war, the end result of which was usually a few bruises but also a lot of excitement for us, and a great deal of amusement for the adult population.

On one occasion there was a near-casualty – 'Ha'ker (Hawker) Lizzie', a tiny woman who lived in a single small room at No. 4 Links Street, and collected rags around the district. As she left her doorway she was caught up in the mêlée and was very nearly bowled over, but fortunately she emerged unscathed, and later we gave her some assistance as she went around the doors.

When a little older, I accompanied parties of children from the street on rowing-boat trips to Old Torry. The little boat, built like a coble and painted in chequered black and white to make it clearly visible to other vessels, set out from the jetty at Fittie during the summer months, carrying passengers across the mouth of the Dee for a halfpenny each. This little outing was very popular with the many children that packed the boat on fine days.

All too soon the cold dark mornings would arrive, and the dark nights in which we would follow the leerie, or lamplighter, as he went his round of the streets, reaching up to each lamp with his long pole and pulling a small lever inside the glass to turn on the gas, which was ignited by a pilot jet. As soon as day came he would go on his round again, turning the lamps off.

I am sure that even in winter no child from the Fittie squares to the furthest point of St Clements can have known the meaning of the word 'boredom'. Homework or not, there was no lack of things to do. On two evenings each week the school 'janny' Mr Robertson (a short, grey-haired man with a beard) kept the steam heat going for an extra couple of hours to warm the building for a Play Group, at which there were games and skipping to music, little playlets, country dancing and raffia work lessons, all supervised by some of the teachers. We went to Band Of Hope meetings at the Salvation Army Citadel in the Castlegate, sitting high up in the gallery and singing lustily to the brass band, the rich tones of which reverberated around the huge auditorium. We saw slide shows of foreign countries and listened to Bible readings from one of the officers. It was an eagerly anticipated evening.

When snow fell and the cold was fierce, those who had sledges hauled them out from their coal cellars and those who had not found pieces of corrugated iron as substitutes. Sometimes we would sledge in Links Street, which was on a slight slope, but Georgie and I found it much more fun to venture with our sledge (made for us, of course, by Grandfather) to the Corn Hillie just in front of the gasworks. The Corn Hillie was perfect for our purposes as it was fairly steep, with a flatter area at the bottom, so that after thudding off the hill we had a nice long slide to the Junior Football Field below. At times of severe frost we tried skating on the frozen shallow pools at the Links, and of course there were snowball battles in the street. These would sometimes become just a little out of hand and leave somebody greetin'.

Later, I joined the Girls Guildry, which was held in the Church Hall in Links Street, and Georgie joined the Boys Brigade, while Andrew and his chums were members of the Salvation Army Pipe Band. Andrew's blowing on the chanter was not appreciated by my grandmother. Cultivation of a fine old art it may have been, but it was banished from her kitchen, only to reappear in ours. One of Andrew's friends was a drummer; his drums were banned in our house, so he rattled his sticks on softer surfaces, but there was no retreat from the chanters!

CHAPTER 4
DEPRESSION YEARS – FRIENDS, HEALTH AND WEALTH.

The far end of Links Street seemed to us quiet and remote, although we knew most of the people who lived there. Walking past them on our frequent excursions to the Links and beach we would be jokingly told 'nae to fa' in the watter the day' or some such thing – frequently we came back from the beach soaking wet after over-enthusiastic wading in the sea. The later nineteenth century brick houses towards the top of the street had unusual arch-shaped doors and windows at street level. Half way along the street were some two-storey houses with a pend leading to the back, where there were stone stairs ascending to flats on the upper floors. The Robb family lived there, and also Kate Morris, who managed to be kind and cheery despite arthritis in her feet that obliged her to wear soft gym-type shoes so that she could hobble along with some measure of comfort.

Also towards the far end of the street lived the Sutherland family whose two sons, Albert and George, were pals of my uncle Andrew. One afternoon they decided to hold a cellar party, to which Andrew brought me along. I was not too impressed; the pressure stove on which they brewed the tea filled the air with oily fumes, giving the banana sandwiches a most peculiar taste, but Andrew and the Sutherland boys seemed to enjoy it all. It was certainly different. Others among the many chums with whom I played in the street were the Mauchline boys, whose father worked as a 'lumper' in the Fish Market. They lived in No. 6, part of the older 'brickers'.

As I have already touched upon, some families, despite the poverty of the times, were very large, putting an increasing strain on already inadequate finances. The Scotts, who lived about midway along the street, were particularly numerous, and no doubt all had to squeeze into two rooms, but at least Mr Scott had a job. He was a professional photographer, and could be seen daily carrying his camera and tripod. His wages cannot have been anything other than meagre, and of course there was no such thing as family allowance, but for all that the Scotts were a happy crew. The Leipers, the Lyons and the Nichols (whose two big lads were rather a nuisance, inclined to bully the younger children) also lived in that part of the street.

In those overcrowded conditions, it was common for children to sleep 'top and bottom' four or more in a bed. Sometimes there would be a bed-wetter in their midst too. Poor housing, large families and lack of facilities were prevalent not only in St Clements but in other areas of the city as well, and malnutrition began to show itself as the Depression dragged on.

When winters became severe, coats and jackets served as additional bed coverings. Fleas ('flechs', as we called them) emerged from the floorboards of old houses to plague the occupants. The battle against them eventually took a decisive turn when Keatings Powder came on the market, but that was still some time away.

The City Fever Hospital was always full, especially of children suffering from contagious diseases. No visitors could be allowed inside, so on visiting days people would be seen conversing with patients through the open windows. Short wooden steps were available so that visitors could have full view of the invalid. No other contact was permitted, so even very young children had to do without a 'bosie' from their tearful mothers, who longed to be able to give them a cuddle.

The chemist's shop was always busy with people seeking 'home remedies'. Common nuisances against which these were used included lice and nits, rife in a society of crowded school classrooms and jampacked homes where little personal privacy was possible and hygiene was poor. On the first sign of either infestation I was sent straight to the chemist, bearing a little jar in which to carry twopence worth of 'quashy chips', a pale amber-coloured liquid with what looked like small chips of wood floating in it. I have no idea what it consisted of, but it was a sure cure. After its use my mother would wash my hair thoroughly with black soap just as an added safety measure.

One day I was sent to the chemist with a small cup to purchase threepence worth of 'California Poppy' perfume for my mother. She was going to a wedding, and she wanted a little scent, which could be bought quite cheaply in this way. The precious drops of liquid were carefully poured into a little scent bottle for storage. Woolworths sold 'Evening In Paris' in attractive small dark-coloured bottles, but these cost 6d. and she preferred 'California Poppy' anyway!

In those difficult times, children and adults must have been blessed with 20-20 vision, as few wore spectacles, although Woolworths sold them cheaply enough. The schools dentist in Diamond Street gave treatment to children, but adults suffered much dental deterioration. Our family had the advantage of a reasonable diet with the fish, buckies and cod roes (or 'ranns') which we could obtain, but such protein-rich foods were not easily accessible to everyone.

Serious accidents were not uncommon in homes where the fireside area was cluttered with clothes, pots, hot kettles, etc. For many, the day of the gas cooker had still to come, and often a freshly-boiled kettle would be taken off the kitchen range or gas ring and set down in the hearth to make room for another utensil. On one tragic occasion a child died after taking a drink from the spout of a hot kettle so placed.

Those in really dire straits could use the Public Soup Kitchen in Loch Street, where I once accompanied a chum when she went for a large jug of soup. Another time, I visited the People's Dispensary, where the girl I was with received a bottle of red-coloured medicine – for bloodlessness, she said. Nobody in our area, working or not, could afford the 3s. or 3s. 6d. that it cost to call a doctor except in an emergency or when an illness became really obstinate or severe, so home remedies were the order of the day. In winter we were given daily doses of cod liver oil emulsion or Virol, and periodic spoonfuls from a jar of sulphur and treacle. A cold or a bad cough ('hoast') was treated by application of camphorated oil to the chest so that the clearing vapour was breathed in, the patient being nourished on gruel. Cuts and bruises were dealt with by Granny, who was very adept with hot poultices. Once, during cairtie time, a rusty nail on one of our vehicles went into my ankle and I developed blood poisoning. The poultices of bread, boiling water and (I think) baking soda were ruthlessly applied on a cloth; though painful, they were effective.

By law, all babies had to be vaccinated for smallpox by the age of six months, but the antibiotic drugs of the present day were unknown. Scarlet fever, tuberculosis ('consumption') and diptheria raged amid the less serious complaints like measles, whooping cough and mumps, which were as common among children as they are now. Diptheria was particularly dangerous; in one of the flats above the St Clements Bar lived a little chum of mine – a boy six or seven years of age, and the only child of middle-aged parents. He had a beautiful large rocking horse on which we played for many an hour, but our friendship was short-lived. One day came the sad news that he had died of this dreaded disease which today has been all but eradicated.

Babies were born at home and were proudly paraded in white knitted shawls, sometimes with a little veil over the face and head as extra decoration (in addition, I suppose, to keeping dust out of the face and eyes). Mothers would have a black woollen carrying shawl, intended for casual use only. My mother knitted both kinds .of shawl, but in our family only the white one was deemed proper attire for going up-town. Black shawls did have other uses, though – warm and cosy, they were very popular among the older women for trips to the rowie-shop on cold mornings!

The weaning of babies on to solids did not take place as early as is the case nowadays. Usually they were breast or bottle fed for the first nine months or so, although sometimes they would be given rolled biscuit or 'flour of meal', the dust from the bottom of the Co-op oatmeal bins, which was very nourishing. Cheap condensed milk (½d. per tin) was clearly labelled 'unfit for babies', but poor families gave it to their infants all the same – they had little choice. One baby in our street took a convulsion and died due, it was said, to excessive temperature during teething.

Some couples in our area began keeping company as soon as they left school at 14, and most people had only one courtship. Money was always a problem. Women were more employable than men as they constituted a source of cheap labour. Young men lucky enough to be serving an apprenticeship were so poorly paid that a fiancée could earn more at 'the fish' or at the likes of 'Tinny Robertson's' in Lemon Street, where my mother and my Aunt Daisy worked at various times, making such articles as oatcake and biscuit tins. To crown it all, many apprentices were paid off on the very day that they became journeymen, rather than have them qualify for full wages. It was therefore a bitter struggle to put any money aside for the future. Some lads left school, courted and married without ever having a job that lasted any time, or indeed without ever having a job at all.

In the St Clements of the 1920s and 1930s, attitudes towards sex were basically Victorian, and the matter was not discussed, particularly in front of children. In our house, adult conversation was carefully guarded and it was only when my mother began crocheting baby things or, in particular, knitting a white shawl, that I knew to expect an addition to the family. I never heard the word 'pregnant' or anything relating to the facts of life, and we were taught nothing about biology at school.

I have heard sex described as 'the only thing that people could have for nothing' in those depressed days, and there is much truth in that saying. Contraception, meanwhile, was a matter of almost universal ignorance and there was little or no discussion about it. Little wonder that families grew. Outwith marriage, there was a strict code of conduct that kept courting couples together, and it was seldom that a quick wedding was found necessary. Promiscuity was not at all common, and was very much frowned upon. Any girl that did end up literally 'holding the baby' would be taken care of by her parents, but that meant another mouth to feed, and such situations were strongly discouraged. No social services or official help were available.

Despite all hardships, I never did hear of ill-treatment of children in our area, even though parents had bairns constantly about them. Good hard smacks on the behind and the occasional dunt on the ear were administered when behaviour got out of hand, but I know of no 'cruel' treatment in those days. I am certain that any such thing would have been very quickly reported to the authorities by neighbours.

The death of a family breadwinner was truly a disaster. The mother of one of my friends, Lottie Walker, was a widow, in very poor circumstances due to the meagreness of the widow's pension at the time – 'ten shilling widows', they were called. Mrs Walker had two other daughters and a son, all young, and they lived in two rooms at No. 6 Links Street. How mothers managed to keep a house and family clean, clothed and fed under conditions like these I do not know, but somehow they did. Mr Walker had been a cooper by trade, but was caught up in the Depression and had been unable to find work. A brain tumour caused the final catastrophe of his death.

Those who died were always laid out at home, there being no funeral rest rooms, and usually a white sheet was hung over the window to intimate a family bereavement. I often went with my grandmother to visit bereaved friends or relations, and there was no shielding of the young in matters of this kind – it was treated as a fact of life. When anyone died in Links Street, every man turned out for the funeral, walking slowly behind the hearse, which was drawn by two black horses with waving black plumes on their heads. The men formed a long column in the narrow street, attired, as a mark of respect, in the suits which they reserved for such occasions.

Early each weekday morning, before the machinery whined into action at the Gourock Rope Works hard by Links Street, we could plainly hear even from indoors a sound like an army on the march as the men of Russell's shipyard walked down the Tarrie to work. At three minutes to eight the shipyard horn would blow, signifying to me that it was time to get up for school. At eight it sounded again, after which all was quiet until the riveters began their clangorous work.

Shipbuilding and fishing were Aberdeen's main industries at that time, and apprenticeship in 'the yards' was a coveted job. Many good lads made their beginnings there on the road to becoming journeymen, among them my uncle Andrew who in 1930, despite the Depression, managed to find employment as an apprentice plater. On Tuesdays he came to my grandmother for dinner at midday, and would give me twopence to go and purchase for him five Club or Woodbine cigarettes from Maggie Caie's. Next I would be sent to Buchan's paper shop for a copy of the magazine 'Red Letter', ordered every week along with 'Funny Wonder' and 'Rover', which came out on Saturdays. As he ate, Andrew would prop up the 'Red Letter' on the sugar bowl to read 'The Red Barn Mystery' while I waited patiently for a turn myself. Unfortunately, I was often disappointed, as he would tuck the paper in the pocket of his old jacket and go off to work with it!

When, that same year, the second *St Sunniva* was being fitted out at the yards, Andrew 'acquired' a soup plate as a souvenir. It was a white plate with a nice blue trim around it and, in the centre, a picture of the ship with the name underneath. He used the plate regularly; one day when the soup was rather on the thin side, there came a complaint – 'Hey, mother, the boatie's floatin'!'

When this beautiful ship was launched, our school 'crocodile' came along to watch the event. It was a great thrill to see the vessel slide smoothly and gracefully into the water, then quietly settle as the large crowd

The first "St. Sunniva" was wrecked in 1930. A new vessel was built at Hall Russell's yard and launched in April 1931.

The building of vessels such as these tugs, "Foremost 81" and "Foremost 82" provided scarce work in the lean years.

*"Hunger-marchers"
became a regular
feature of the
Depression Years.*

An unemployed workers' procession, 1932.

cheered. How sad to hear of its sinking during the second World War.

As the world recession took effect, the sound of the shipyard men's footsteps on the Tarrie became fainter and fainter. Soon shipwrights, caulkers, riveters and other skilled workers from the St Clements area could be seen wandering on the Links or sitting propped against the wall at the top of Links Street, feet stretched out on the pavement, playing cards for matches. They already had the abject look of the unemployed of the time, for they knew that to be on the Broo meant poverty. For them and their families there loomed desperate visions of the Parish.

At the Labour Exchange in Market Street men stood in allocated numbered queues (which they nicknamed 'Trap 1' and 'Trap 2') to sign on. Some worked for two weeks, then went back on the Broo for the next fortnight. Casual labour was engaged on a daily basis to unload cargo ships as they berthed in the harbour. A crowd of men would gather and the lucky ones would be chosen, leaving the rest disappointed and not a little resentful at having to resort to such tactics to obtain a day's work. A man from Links Street went with some friends to the harbour one day when news came that the flour boat had arrived. Somehow they managed to 'get in', and all day his friends guided him through the hard task of unloading heavy sacks of flour, a job of which he had no experience at all. He went home triumphantly with his pay, which he considered well worth the aches in every muscle and the skin peeling from his back!

There were occasions when even we children, as we roamed free as the wild birds, were brought face to face with the realities of life in the Depression. Some people broke under the extreme financial pressure to which they were subjected, and we saw one elderly woman in Links Street being carried to an ambulance from her home, where, in penniless misery and with her husband away at sea, she had finally tried to gas herself. One man threw himself into the harbour; he was pulled out unharmed, but not so another whose lifeless form we saw lying under a tarpaulin at the foot of the harbour steps. Grim pictures, but soon put from our young minds as we played in the street and attended school together with an innocence which, looking back on it, was a precious thing. We were happy children even though some of us, girls and boys, were constrained to wear the calf-length tacketty-soled boots of the Parish.

Ownership of such things as gramophones and radios was far from universal in St Clements even in the 1930s, and a favourite way of whiling away the time was in the art of conversation – gossip, in fact. It was, I suppose, hardly surprising that some couples should quarrel and shout at each other when anger and frustration got the better of them, but the noise could often be plainly heard in the street, and such episodes were the very stuff of stair-head or kitchen tattle. Other subjects might be what the minister said when he called, or which horse the scaffie said to back the next day. Sometimes it was 'D'ye ken fa got a job?' or 'how much a Fittie wifie spent in the Copie the day'. Someone's health, a death or a new bairn were all popular topics for dissemination and comment.

Outside the arched York Street entrance to Neptune Terrace, women chatted as they knitted. Some of them were very expert knitters, especially a Mrs Blair who made the most beautiful lacy white baby shawls. They could speak more softly now that the riveters in the shipyard across the street were all but silent. Further along York Street, the Neptune Bar still had a few regulars in its dark interior, although most of its trade now came from the crews of ships in the harbour close by. In those days the building was of two storeys, a nice cosy hostelry where the locals could enjoy a glass of beer while perhaps listening to crewmen's stories of the sea – a subject familiar to the Fittie men who built the ships and sailed in them.

Monday mornings were the busiest time for the pawnshop at the top of Commerce Street. In those times of want and poverty, the sign of three brass balls jutting out over the pavement was a common one. During school holidays some families sent out their older children (most often the girls) with items of value. These always seemed to be wrapped in brown paper without string, and to be fairly bulky so that they had to be carried with both arms out in front. A fair assumption could usually be made as to where they were bound. We were fortunate enough never to have to resort to such measures, but along with friends I did see the inside of the shop, a strange place full of dark wood and thick patterned glass. Upstairs was a counter sectioned off to allow some privacy. Articles were proffered, valued, and exchanged for money and a pawn ticket. They could be redeemed by repayment of the amount within a given time, otherwise they were sold off. Those who were short of ready money could sell their pawn tickets, and it was possible to build up quite a lucrative trade in these.

Bookies' runners were common in the area, a 'flutter' on the horses constituting a little piece of illegal excitement. A betting slip (signed pseudonymously, of course) would be surreptitiously handed to that certain man on the street corner. Bets amounted only to coppers or a threepenny piece, but the man who was rescued from the harbour was a 'runner' who was thought not to have returned his slips and money. I can only surmise that the small sum in his possession was used for some desperate need at home, as he was otherwise of excellent character, a non-drinker and a good father to his large family. Like so many, he was unable to find regular work.

From time to time, quiet spots near the 'big logs' and beside the Broad Hill were the scene of illegal Pitch And Toss schools. Even this relatively innocuous game of tossing pennies came under the heading of illicit gaming, and a look-out had to be posted to watch for the police, any sign of whom would send the men scurrying off.

If life was hard in Britain during the Depression, the law was not ignored. Severe punishments were meted out to criminals – the birch, hard labour, execution for murder, etc, and whether or not by reason of this, violent crime was unknown on the terrifying scale of today. Links Street was part of the extensive beat of just one policeman who patrolled most of the area. We had great respect for the bobby, who went through dark passageways with a torch to make certain no doors to, for instance, Jock Wood's shop or the pub had been tampered with. There were never any break-ins that I heard of. We never answered back to the bobby when ordered to go home from the quayside or the harbour where we were playing – to do so was to provoke a good hard kick on the backside!

However bad the times, a smoke was a much-favoured indulgence, and men could be seen gathering their cigarette stubs into old tobacco tins, using the remaining flakes of tobacco to roll another. The cheapest cigarettes, at five for twopence, were Woodbine or Club. Cigarette cards, given with the slightly more expensive brands, were much in vogue and were enthusiastically collected and traded. With Ardath brand came coupons which could be saved for gifts such as household dishes or towels, but I never knew of anyone but my Uncle Andy who could afford this make.

Tea wrappers and packets were another source of gifts. My father ordered large quantities of Blue And Gold tea for his ship's stores, and would save up the coupons. After a few trips he would take us along to a shop in King Street to claim our goods – a welcome windfall, as we could never have bought the brand ourselves, certainly not in pounds or half-pounds; loose dry goods from the Co-op were our limit.

At the Links end of Cotton Street, by the foot of what is now the Beach Boulevard, no-one could miss (by sight or smell) the black, brick-built bulk of the gasworks. Between Cotton Street and Bannermill Street were the City Corn Mills, and farther round the Links was Sandilands Chemical Works, both contributing their own pungence to all that permeated the atmosphere in that quarter of town. When the wind blew westerly the ozone-seekers on the promenade received something rather different from what they expected. The St Clements area was perfectly placed to receive full benefit of every noxious odour, and a regular part of conversation there was 'The gasworks is afa' the day!'

For the children of the district, however, the gasworks provided a modest source of wealth. Cinders could be purchased from the works for 9d. per sack, but material considered useless was simply dumped in mounds near the Links. Poking around with sticks in these mounds, we would fill pails with whatever usable cinders we could find, picking the burnable ones from among the useless 'danders'. This was good fun, and there was always a crowd of children there, not only from the surrounding streets but from closer to town as well. Cairties were invaluable for transport. The cinders, which could be used to eke out a coal fire, were always welcome at home, and a pailful would bring a small financial reward.

Jobless many may have been, but still boys had aspirations as to what they wished to do after that distant day when they would leave school. Employment with the Post Office was very difficult to obtain, but at least one of our group fancied the job of telegram boy, pedalling around town on a bright red push-bike. One or two had ideas about joining the Merchant Navy, visiting different countries. All sorts of ambitions were voiced, but most favoured was apprenticeship at a trade, however poorly paid.

Even though women's wages were less than journeymen's, girls would sooner work in the fish houses, the Glove Factory in Rose Street, Tinny Robertson's, etc than in shops, where the pay was worse still. Some girls found jobs 'in service', working as maids in the larger West End houses where they could 'live in' and be fed as part of their remuneration. Many, especially from Fittie and Old Torry, worked as fish net braiders, and hardy characters they were. The girls from the Fittie Squares, with whom I was later to work, thought nothing of walking in all weathers, four times a day, all the way to Albert Quay, across the lock gate bridge at Wellington Street and through the Fish Market to Point Law. My grandfather also walked to work every day, whatever the weather, along the quays and across Regent Bridge. But life was not all toil – there were popular pastimes and entertainments too.

CHAPTER 5
AMUSEMENTS, HIGH DAYS, HOLIDAYS – AND OTHER DAYS.

During the early 1930s there grew a great fad for whist drives, which were held in halls all over the city. The game was taken very seriously, some developing quite a mania for it, and anyone who 'reneged' was likely to go home with a very red face. Without doubt, though, the most popular pastime available to all was picture-going, for which the introduction of talkies brought a new enthusiasm. Even in the worst of the Depression queues could be seen outside Aberdeen's cinemas every night as patrons sought a brief escape from the pressures and deprivations of daily life. To go to the cinema was to lose oneself for an hour or so in a land of glamorous stars where the sun always shone warm and bright. Musicals proved popular as soon as talkies arrived, and there also appeared films like 'King Kong' and 'Dracula' to thrill and scare their avid audiences. One night, my mother and I went to see 'Dracula' at the Starrie. Shouts of 'Watch yer back!' went up as our fellow patrons endeavoured to help the unsuspecting victims on the screen. Walking home afterwards we nonchalantly shared a bag of chips from the chip-shop in Wales Street, but neverthless we 'watched our backs' in the darkness until we reached the safety of Links Street!

As a pre-school child, I was taken regularly to the Starrie's Saturday matinees, and thus became as devoted a film-goer as any. A penny from my grandfather was an essential part of the funding of my visit each Saturday to the 'tuppenny rush', as the matinee was known. One penny came from my mother, earned by washing dishes and carrying out other chores. When Granda came back from work I would cross the landing to await my other penny from him. Of course he knew perfectly well the reason for my visit, but he would never say so. He would eat his dinner, sit down in his chair by the fire, pick up the 'Funny Wonder' and carefully extract the page containing the exploits of Cowboy Charlie. As he read, he would carefully roll a piece of tobacco, fill his pipe, light it in a slow and leisurely fashion, then put the little metal lid in place and puff contentedly. 'Granda', I would say, 'I'm ga'n' t' the Starrie'. 'Aye? Fit's on the day?' With an anxious eye on the church clock, which we could see through the window, I would tell him. He would then carefully draw some coppers from his pocket and, as 2 p.m. ticked ever closer, slowly and deliberately select a penny, which he gave to me. It was a weekly ritual, a game which he enjoyed in an impish way – he was a dear man.

In the cinema we merely tolerated romantic films in which the hero and heroine kissed and spoke about love – at the Starrie we would hiss these scenes until they changed to something more to our liking! No such

63

behaviour was tolerated at the nearby Casino, Wales Street. A popular cinema with nice subdued lighting, heavy stage drapes and good quality coverings on the floor and stairs, it was much posher than the 'Starrie', but to us it was not half as much fun.

On high days and holidays, and at just about any other time, a visit to the cinema made the most popular treat. Each Hogmanay, whatever the day of the week (excepting Sundays, of course), there was a special matinee to which, with some thankfulness, any mother who could scrape twopence together packed off her children so that some housework could be done in readiness for the evening's guests. The Starrie was usually full to capacity, the smell of oranges filling the air. This very basic little cinema was sometimes derisively referred to as the 'Flechy Starrie', but for us it was a haven – an escape into the land of cowboys and glamorous film stars. In silent film days, before I was able to read the captions and blurbs that came up on the screen, I would constantly pester Andrew and Georgie with 'Fit dis that say?' The two boys would send me to the ladies' toilet, to search in the waste bin for discarded pieces of film which were sometimes dumped there. These were put together for a little cinematograph machine that Andrew had, and with which periodically he would give a 'private show', the wall of the bed recess acting as a screen and the curtains around it giving the appropriate air of authenticity. As the family sat 'at the pictures' I would walk around with a torch as the attendant or 'checker'. The clips were mainly from comedy films featuring the great stars of the time, but some patience was required by the audience as the pieced-together snippets kept coming apart and having to be rejoined.

The Starrie's checkers had rather a hard time during special matinees thanks to the Hogmanay present of an apple and an orange that was given to each child on admission. Orange peel and apple cores were pelted on them by the rowdier elements, and before long the management resorted to presenting the fruit on the way out!

At home, meanwhile, last -minute preparations were in progress, and on return from the pictures we would be sent to Hunter's, next to Davidson's paper shop at the top of Church Street, to fetch vegetables for soup. The owner of this little shop was a small red-cheeked man who always wore a cloth cap. We had an eye for his home-made candy apples, his tray candy which he broke expertly with a tiny hammer, and his puff candy, the best that I have ever tasted. Georgie and I usually bought some of the latter after putting the vegetables in the message bag and paying with a silver threepenny piece – 'two pennyworth of veg and a penny for ga'n''.

The pubs in the area would be filling with men soon after evening opening time. The St Clements (my grandfather's venue), the Fittie Bar in Wellington Street, the Neptune in York Street, the Ancient Bar in Church Street and the quayside bars all did brisk trade on that special night that is

Christmas time brought delight for some, but not for all.

The "feein market", 1932 – complete with itinerant street musician.

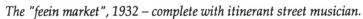

St. Clement's Church, 1970's. The tower pinnacles were removed for safety but were being restored in December 1992.

In early 1928 the original "Tarry Briggie" over the railway at Fish Street was replaced. In the background is West St. Clement's church.

so dear to the hearts of Scots everywhere. The quayside pubs would generally be well patronised by foreign seamen eager to go ashore from their ships for a little while, if only to have a change of faces from those surrounding them from day to day.

In the tenements, those who could afford to do so made broth, the delicious smell of which pervaded the stairways as final touches were added to the evening's arrangements. The last day of the old year saw the harbour filled to capacity as trawlers raced to port and cargo ships tied up at the quayside. Trawl fishermen with sea bags on their shoulders could be seen quickly making their way home to have a rest, or, in the case of the later arrivals, to get there before the bells. No doubt some stopped at a watering-hole for a quick drink before closing time at 9 o'clock.

In our kitchen in Links Street, everything had been made clean and shining. I was allowed to stay up, marvelling at how coal, usually carefully conserved, was still being put on the fire at 9 or 10 o'clock at night. A new piece of American oil-cloth adorned the kitchen table, its bright shiny pattern adding cosiness to the scene. Soon the bottle of tawny port wine, the cheese, the sultana cake and the shortbread would be placed on the table together with some glasses. At Granny's across the stair landing, the same preparations were under way. Georgie and I were dispatched 'ben the room' – Granny's front room where, by a big cheery fire in the grate, we sat reading comics and roasting chestnuts.

At 9 o'clock Georgie and I would hear the closing bell at the St Clements Bar across the street, and shortly after that Granda would come up the stairs, quite cheerful after a nip or two and a pint of beer. Normally a very moderate, quiet, mild-natured man, he would annoy my Granny with his chatter, especially when he began to call her 'Muggie'. Margaret was her name, and she did not like being called anything else. He would praise her volubly, saying, 'You're as good as gold, Muggie', and when he attempted to rise out of his chair by the corner of the kitchen fireplace she would give him a little push back. Oh how Granny detested the drink.

On the stroke of the church clock at midnight, the siren of every ship in the harbour began to sound in a booming welcome to the New Year. To the noise of the sirens, the bottles were opened and a Guid New Year was wished to everyone. Georgie and I were each given a glass of fruit wine, and then there began a tour of the tenement with mother and father. Upstairs, Charlie Riddel, father of a large grown-up family, danced the Highland Fling and Molly his daughter played the mandoline (a musical craze of the time). Beldie down on the ground floor, the Rennie family, the Browns on the floor above, all were visited to exchange greetings on a night when the hardships of life were forgotten together with any ill feeling or differences among neighbours. My father sang 'Wi' My Big Kilmarnock Bonnet' and 'Auld Scots Mother O' Mine', and would bring tears to the eyes of his listeners with 'Scotland I Adore Thee' as he became increasingly maudlin. Granny sang 'The Bonnie Wee Windae', and Granda would begin 'The Tay Bridge Disaster', which was the signal for bedtime for the younger fry. Usually before the last verse of this long, sad song I was asleep. Hope for a good New Year was in everybody's heart – hope, perhaps, for work for the workless, or just for better times. As folk so succinctly remarked, 'It couldna get worse, could it?'

Christmas was a very much quieter affair. Seated in our classroom in St Clement Street school, we always knew when it was coming - the lights in the Co-op windows opposite would be draped round with red crêpe paper, giving everything a rosy glow. In school the carols would begin – 'I Saw Three Ships Come Sailing In', 'Good King Wenceslas', 'The First Noel'. Santie might be coming to fill stockings with perhaps a sugar mouse, a toy from Woolies and a penny in the toe (if the family could afford it), but apart from these small things Christmas Day was not much celebrated in Scotland at that time. Those who were in employment had to work as usual, leaving festivities for Hogmanay.

When my brother James McInnes junior was born, I was allowed to rock him in the wooden cradle that my grandfather had made for me, his first grandchild. The cradle was sturdily built, with a hood, and with a small wooden knob at either side. To either of those knobs my mother would tie a length of string, thus allowing her to rock the cradle while she lay in bed! As James grew bigger, he began to tag along with me when I went out to play. When we bought milk from the milkman, he loved to feed the horse with pieces of bread. One day, after having done so, he became fascinated with the tap on the milk urn, and before anyone could stop him he turned it on. The milk spilled out on to the road and my mother was summoned. She placated the man by giving him some fish; 'Onywey, it wis the skim milk', he said, and little James was forgiven.

On another occasion our James spotted a large fish which was about to fall from a dray heading up Links Street to the salters. It lay tail downwards, and a quick pull brought it tumbling into his arms. He ran with his prize through the lobby to the wash-house, where later the fish was washed, cleaned and cut into steaks. More than one family had fish for supper that night.

I looked forward to the time when I could take James to school, but instead of going to St Clement Street he had to go to York Street School (by the Neptune Bar and just opposite the shipyards), which was taking in overspill pupils that summer. His first day there remained imprinted on my mother's memory for long afterwards – screaming and protesting, he clung fast to the railings outside. Once inside, however, he was soothed with sweets and kind words by the teacher Miss Crombie and the headmistress, and after that he was happier. Grandmother knitted him a new 'gansey' (jersey) and bought him a school bag to stop his daily complaints about the place. Thus encouraged, he went along quietly with the other five year-olds.

One day, he answered a knock on our door. On the doorstep was a woman who looked at him and announced, 'Manage' (pronounced French-style with the accent on the second syllable). James shouted to mother, 'Ma, Mrs Manage wants ye!' A manage or 'tiddley' was a sort of money club into which, say, ten members put a small amount of money each week and drew numbers to win the week's takings, which might amount to ten florins– a fair sum then. I do not know where the name 'tiddley' originated for this method of saving; the only other use of the word of which I am aware is as a naval expression, 'tiddley suit', for a best uniform.

Weddings were always grand occasions. Whether or not the bride wore white (traditional, but rather expensive for many), the sight of a taxi would attract a small crowd, confetti at the ready. One of the wedding party – usually the bride's father – would throw 'scramble' coppers for the kids to retrieve from the roadway.

When I was about four years old, my Aunt Daisy married a lad named Andy from 'up the toon'. A big genial man, Andy was second fisherman on a trawler of which his father was skipper. Attired in his best checked tweed plus-fours (then very fashionable and particularly associated with golfers) he would call on Daisy to take her out.

A real toff was Andy. Daisy, meanwhile, was petite and fair-haired, unlike my mother, who was tall and dark. On her wedding day she wore a short knee-length blue silk 'flapper-style' dress with an overlay of the same material cut in petal-shaped sections and trimmed with silver thread. A blue silk cloche hat, cream coloured shoes with pointed toes, and matching handbag and gloves completed her outfit. We missed Daisy when she and Andy went to live in Torry; just as much we missed the big boxes of chocolates that Andy brought, which usually lay on the table in the front room and from which we children had many a surreptitious treat. Also gone were the pennies that Andy gave me before he and Daisy went off to the pictures, the childish fun that Georgie and I had shouting 'Andy, Andy, canna mak' candy' through the keyhole as the couple sat by the front room fire, and the pleasure of holding the hand-mirror as Daisy skilfully finger-waved her hair after washing it. I am glad to say that at more than 80 years of age Daisy is still slim and youthful-looking.

On my ninth birthday I had a little party to which I invited a few girls and boys from Links Street. My best friend was Olive Fowler from No. 1, where she lived with seven brothers and sisters and her parents in two small rooms at the top of the house. Olive's father had nice curly auburn hair, while her mother had very straight pale auburn hair which she wore in a bun at the back of her head. Half of the family had the curly auburn, and the other half the straight.

To provide a party treat my father borrowed the small ice cream freezer from his ship, and Georgie and I were sent to the ice-making company on Waterloo Quay to fetch a bass bag full of ice pieces, costing twopence. The custard was made and poured into a metal canister, which was then placed in the small wooden tub. The ice was packed around it and everyone took a turn at the handle, making the canister revolve until the ice cream was ready. Andrew, who was by then in his teens, brought his girl friend Nellie and two of his pals, who also brought girls along. They had fun playing 'Postman's Knock, 'Bottlie' and other kissing games while we enjoyed ourselves with 'The Grand Old Duke Of York'. Our home-made ice cream was excellent.

Early one summer Saturday morning, Grandmother came into our house informing us that we were all going on a subbie outing to Cults. She was in 'formal' attire – her good grey coat and a new matching velour hat with deep upturned brim, gun-metal coloured silk stockings (standard wear for the middle-aged or elderly woman in those days) and black suede shoes. Quickly my mother made herself ready, and the necessary ablutions for the family (now including my new baby brother John) were put into motion. All of a sudden there was a noise and a loud exclamation from my grandmother. A piece of ceiling plaster had broken off and was now adorning her nice new hat, filling it to the brim, so to speak. A stunned silence, then gales of laughter from everyone.

At last we arrived at Cults, and after a stroll around the village we were taken by Grandmother to a tea shop for a treat. It was quite a novelty to sit at a table with a white tablecloth and be served tea and a large plate of fancy cakes by a real waitress. Such occasions were few and far between, and we did our best to enjoy this one to the full, even though we knew that we were under Grandmother's ever-critical eye, with a compression of the lips or an almost imperceptible shake of the head a warning to behave. Nevertheless, it was a good day out, and, did we but realise as much at the time, it involved the expenditure of several precious shillings from Grandmother's purse.

I was my grandmother's regular companion at St Clement's Church on Sundays, and on the many occasions when she went to visit her sister Bess and Daisy and a brother in Torry. We would do the social round together, walking there and back. Even when I was quite small she would take me to church and I would sit with her in her pew in the gallery. For sitting quietly I would be rewarded with a pandrop, popped straight into my mouth in case I dropped it on the floor and made a noise. 'Sook it, dinna crunch it!' Granny would be dressed in her Sunday best – black astrakhan coat, velour hat, black shoes and handbag, and the inevitable gun-metal coloured stockings. She always wore a necklace – 'It keeps my neck warm!', she would say. After the service she would stop for a short blether with her sisters Mary Jane and Bess; one Sunday I ended up in trouble because, apparently, I stared for too long at Auntie Bess. She was wearing a black hat with a thick veil fixed beneath her chin. I had never seen a hat like it before and found it quite intriguing! Ladies would never enter church bareheaded, and Sunday School girls wore hats too.

Congregations were predominantly female, and for church-going the only way to dress was in one's Sunday best. Those who could not afford Sunday clothes were, in effect, debarred from coming to church. To attempt it would not have been the done thing, and would have led to being very much looked down upon, a situation which I considered disgraceful. Of course, it was also true that many did not attend church simply because they disliked sitting through the long, solemn, Calvinistic sermons!

Church services were for adults only, with occasionally a sprinkling of children who could be relied upon by their accompanying elders to behave themselves and sit quietly. Most of us went to the church hall, where we sang our Sunday School hymns and learned our little texts. Grandmother bought my sister and I a little fourpenny paperback hymn book, and the first hymn that she taught us was, typically, 'O What Can Little Hands Do'. She was so much against our having 'idle hands'. Once in my pre-school days she took me to a Mother's Meeting 'jist for company', and throughout the evening sat knitting and knitting pairs of socks!

The Crombie family of Grandholm Mills were life-long members of St Clement's Church, and I remember one of the Misses Crombie playing the piano and rehearsing the junior choir. Another was head teacher at York Street School. The church's last minister, Rev. Arthur Jones, was inducted in 1964, and the dwindling congregation, attending services even after they had moved to other parts of the city, remained loyal until St Clement's finally closed in 1986. Five hundred years after the first chapel was built on the site, the church lies disused and desolate, the tower minus its stone pinnacles which were taken down after storm damage, and its small churchyard mossy and neglected. But two faces of its clock are still illuminated at night, and the third face (black with gilt numerals, and probably very old) still looks towards where Links Street stood.

In our household, Monday was wash-day – our turn to use the wash-house outside in the backie. In those days before the advent of automatic washing machines, biological wash-powders, wool softeners, etc, the washing of clothes was rather a mammoth task. It began as soon as the

71

family had been dispatched to school and work. First my grandmother would light the fire under the clothes boiler, a standard piece of equipment in wash-houses everywhere, consisting of a large copper with a fire hearth below it, encased in a whitewashed brick surround. Next, my mother would bring down all the dirty laundry plus the youngest child, who had to be supervised.

Attached to the wall were two large square wooden tubs, each with a cold water tap. Near the door was a round wooden tub, also with a tap. This was used for rinsing – in cold water, of course; the only hot water came from the clothes boiler in the corner. Over the copper was a thick wooden cover (to keep the heat in), and in the front of the brickwork was a little iron door with the fireplace behind it. On the opposite wall was a big mangle with an unwieldy wooden handle and huge wooden rollers.

Armed with a scrubbing brush (which resembled a currying brush used in the grooming of horses), washboards, Kilty soap, Hudson's Powder and a block of chloride of lime, my mother set about the washing. I hated wash-days, an attitude shared by my grandfather, whose arrival from work at lunchtime was considered an interruption. He would look balefully at his plate of boiled beef (from Sunday's soup) and potatoes, and pass remarks about poor midday meals on Mondays, but nothing that Grandfather said ever daunted my grandmother!

I would arrive home at midday from St Clement Street School, and after a quick, scant dinner would be expected to take the current baby out in the carrying shawl for an airing. While doing this, I would keep a close eye on the church clock, which faced the door of our house, and whenever the long lunch break (12 o'clock to 2) was over I would dash thankfully back to the haven of school until 4 p.m. For those still toiling in the wash-house there were many chores left to do, but eventually everything was cleared and left neat and tidy, and I would help to carry the baskets of wet clothes up to the loft at the top of the tenement for drying. The loft was a large attic room with a clean, bare wooden floor and a fireplace. A fire was lit in the grate, and ropes stretched the length of the room from hooks on the walls. The wet clothes were then hung up, and the wash day was over.

From the stair landing window to the the top of the wash-house chimney there ran a pulley rope, but this was very short and was used only on sunny days for clothes that were difficult to dry. The mangle, for all its unwieldiness, did not succeed in removing much water, and eventually my mother invested in her first labour-saving device – an Acme wringer!

By that time I, like most elder girls in a family, was being given housework to do. This included scrubbing the stairs, at which I was apparently satisfactory, as a young woman who lived upstairs with her elderly mother paid me a shilling a time to do her 'turn' for her. She worked in an office, and did not care to perform this rather menial task, but I did not mind it – most girls, after all, had such chores to do. The cleaning of brasses was another duty that frequently fell to me. It took much time and patience, and on a Friday night I, and often my sister too, would be fully occupied making all the brassware and fittings shine. And of course we always had to wash the dishes.

Every night I would clean the children's shoes ready for school the next day. It came as something of a relief when, during the summer holidays, soft canvas shoes or bare feet became the order of the day. My mother's expression for shoe polish was the generic one of 'blake' (black), and if she wanted a tin of brown Cherry Blossom it was 'broon blake'! Girls were expected to help in the wash-house, especially if their mother was expecting yet another baby. Boys, on the other hand, never (in our family at least) had to wash the dishes or clean the house. They did have to carry coal and chop sticks for the fire, but for the most part it was a man's world.

Young women who, by choice or otherwise, were 'left on the shelf' usually became responsible for looking after their parents when the other members of the family had left home. Many had not only to work in order to earn a salary, but also had to nurse an old, ill mother or father – sometimes both. Fortunately, neighbours were willing helpers, if only to look in now and then during the day, to see to the coal fire or perhaps to make a cup of tea. My mother told me that after the first World War many young women remained unmarried simply because of the massacre of so many young men.

Soon after my Aunt Daisy and her husband Andy were married, Andy bought a second-hand motorcycle. Out for a spin in the country one day, they found a place with bushes full of raspberries, and soon we, together with our berry-baskets, were on our way there by bus. We alighted in a small village just outside town, Andy using the pillion seat on his bike to ferry volunteers to the spot. The sight is still with me of my sprightly Grandmother astride the pillion, being 'hurled' along the country lane at some speed. 'My', she exclaimed when her feet touched terra firma once again, 'But that wis rare fun!'

My grandmother had a word or words for every situation. Any dirty-looking character was a 'full mach'. I would be instructed to 'stop plouterin'' when splashing about in water, and when angry she would call me a 'faggot' or a 'nickum'. She would conclude some sad tale or lament with 'Och aye, it's nae lachin' (it's no laughing matter), a phrase often heard among the older women. Another favourite word was 'claik', used as a noun for a gossiping person or as a verb for the act of gossiping. Grandmother was 'black affrontit' when someone or something offended her, someone clumsy or inept was 'fushionless', and after hard work she was absolutely 'connacht'.

Even more noticeable in those days than now was the habit, in the Aberdeen Doric, of adding 'ie' to the end of nouns to give a sort of diminutive – boatie, shoppie, loonie, quinie, etc. Equally prevalent in some parts of town, including our own, was the addition or substitution of 'er' or 'ers', so that the Torry Cinema became the 'Torryers', the Castlegate the 'Castler' and Links Street the 'Linker'. Among teenagers, an enjoyable evening at the dancing or a good film would often be referred to as 'jist mustard', the word 'caker' was popular even then for something very easy, and a 'bosker' was something really excellent. A popular phrase of the time was 'hard as Henderson's', the rather early completed version of which did not bear out the explanation that I received, of its referring to the products of a city baker's firm!

On Friday mornings the real Buchan tongue could be heard in the environs of Hadden Street as farmers congregated in 'boorachies' to talk shop after the market. The brogue was attractive but quite unintelligible to us toon folk who spoke the citified version, itself divided into 'up-the-toon' and 'doon-the-toon'.

CHAPTER 6
UP THE TOON

A small corporation bus ran on a regular service through the town from Fittie to Torry, but we never travelled on it. A trip with mother to George Street (or ' George's Street', as she called it) was always on foot, following the standard route along St. Clement Street to where it opened out into the 'square' flanked by Church Street, Baltic Place and Garvock Wynd, then round into Miller Street, passing Prince Regent Street, Yeats' Lane and Cotton Street, and on to the 'Tarrie Briggie', which was considered to mark the boundary of Fittie. Past Fish Street and St. Clements UF Church (West St. Clements), Commerce Street School and into Commerce Street itself. On the right, opposite the barracks, was the famous 'Cocky' Hunter's original second-hand store, with its motto 'We Sell Everything From a Needle To an Anchor'. There was always a record playing over a loudspeaker at the door, and we heard all about 'Old Faithful – we roam the range together', the latest cowboy song. Behind Commerce Street School is a small hill called the Heading Hill. It has houses at the top, and in those days was quite steep and grassy. On the grass grazed a solitary goat, tethered by a rope. We seldom saw animals apart from domestic pets or horses, so this was quite a novelty.

Past the pawnshop at the top of Commerce Street (there was no Beach Boulevard in those days), and across King Street to the little shops of Queen Street. But before King Street came East North Street, Aberdeen's 'skid row' in which the seamy side of life was more than evident. Aberdeen has always possessed its share of vagrants (referred to in those days simply as 'tramps'), and so it was that each night the Model Lodging House in East North Street opened its grimy Edwardian doors to provide bed and shelter for the homeless. This sanctuary, for such it was, received the usual local abbreviation to its name, being known as the 'Modeler' (or 'Moddler'!). Every morning its unfortunate denizens, their entire wordly possessions clutched in a paper bag or gunny sack, would come out to face another day on the streets.

The street also harboured a population of men and women who could frequently be seen lying about the pavements in a state of near-oblivion. These were the 'feekie drinkers,' a term derived no doubt from the word 'fake' as spoken in the vernacular – to 'feek' something was to cover it up or to disguise it as something else. Desperate alcoholics, they would drink methylated spirit, Brasso, anything. Some specialised in what was referred to as 'fairy wine', prepared by breaking the mantle on a tenement lobby gas light, attaching a rubber tube to the burner, turning the gas on and bubbling it into a bottle of milk. The resulting cocktail they drank.

Woolworths at that time sold large sixpenny bottles of cologne or lavender water, and I remember being instructed, during a spell as assistant in the George Street branch, not to sell this product to a 'feekie'. Poor dregs of humanity, they were easily recognised by their gunny sack on their shoulder and their gaunt, emaciated appearance.

As an alternative route to town, one could bear left at the St. Clement Street 'square' and go along Prince Regent Street to Canal Terrace, which was bounded on the South by the railway goods yard, Waterloo Station. Further towards town, Yeats (pronounced 'Yetts') Lane ran between Miller Street and Canal Terrace. Many families lived in its tenement dwellings, but now everything has vanished and no-one would suspect that it ever existed. The openness of Canal Terrace made this a very pleasant walk on a sunny day.

Broad Street, paradoxically, was not broad at all but very narrow and busy. Camerons, near the corner of the Netherkirkgate, was a shop in which my mother liked to browse, carrying as it did a multitude of materials and other goods. George Street was full of shops, people, the clanging of tramcars and the heady smell of the fruit market. The trams took up most of the narrow roadway, on to which pedestrians spilled from the crowded pavements. The area was a shopper's paradise for those of limited (and perhaps not so limited) means, with prices considerably lower than those on Union Street. True, the quality of goods tended to be correspondingly lower, but with money so scarce people had to be content with what they could afford. Woolworths' George Street store ('Little Woolies') was always busy, especially on a Saturday, its popularity enhanced by the fact that unlike the large Union Street shop it was all on one floor. It sold 'Nothing Over 6d.', but the variety of goods that it stocked made it quite an Aladdin's cave.

Then there were Raggie Morrison's and the Equitable (always pronounced 'Equitable'), where good bargains were to be found on all manner of things ranging from artificial silk stockings to sheets, enamel pails and basins. At Reid & Pearson's could be bought such things as hats, artificial flowers for weddings, ladies lingerie, and fully fashioned silk stockings. The latter cost 2s.lld. (15p) per pair, which we thought rather dear as Raggie Morrison's and the Equitable sold stockings (albeit of lesser quality) for only 7½d!

There were the Mascot and Parkinson's dress shops, Coopers for dairy foods, the fruit bazaar, then in Loch Street the 'Copie' with its comfortable arcade. Further along George Street was the large Isaac Benzies ('I.B.'s') – the choice was enormous as all these shops vied for custom and competed in prices. Other popular emporia were Lawson's and the Star, where our school clothes were bought, as were our wellington boots each winter.

Shopping on a budget – 'Raggie' Morrison's advertise their wares in July 1931.

'Copie' fashion, 1934

Silk hose at half-a-crown, 1934

Advertisement for an uptown store, 1931

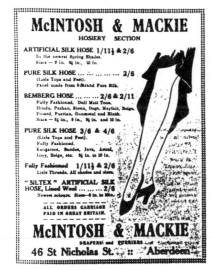

Divi day at the Loch Street 'Copie', May 1929.

"Timmer Market"......1931.

*Most of the "timmer" element has disappeared – crowds
however still flocked round the stalls.*

The last of the old Timmer Markets, 1935. Thereafter the Market moved to Justice Street.

A walk 'roon the Castler', 1935.

Clothing and shoes were usually priced at just under the round sum; a price tag with 19s.11d. on it always looked more enticing than one with £1, and just as now psychological selling techniques were used in shops everywhere. Prices counted in guineas (21s.) instead of pounds could also be found, but these were almost exclusively the preserve of the higher priced clothing and furniture stores.

Working girls could buy dresses for as little as 8s.11d. Dance dresses were available for 21s. or 30s., but that was more than a week's wages and had to be carefully saved. Goods in large fashion stores were generally beyond the means of the George Street shoppers, who preferred to go where, in response to the 'Can I help you?' of the enthusiastic sales assistant, they could reply 'I'm jist lookin' without being made to feel uncomfortable.

The advent of the 1930s brought changes in ladies fashions, as was clearly demonstrated on our cinema screens. Gone was the short 'flapper' dress, the flat bosom and the cloche hat of the previous decade. Now skirts were longer and more flowing, made of such materials as flower-patterned silk. Bosoms were back in vogue, and hats were smaller, neater and flatter. Small-brimmed ones were made for everyday use while wide-brimmed 'picture hats' constituted more formal attire. Wide-legged beach pyjamas, usually in bright coloured cotton, came into fashion, but though popular were not 'easy to wear' and did not suit all of the girls that bought them. Materials used to create the new fashions in women's clothing varied from rich velvets and pure wools to light frothy tulle, georgette, crepe-de-chine, voile satin, taffeta and luxurious pure silk. Evening gowns and dresses made from these were elegant and feminine. Underwear usually had trims of ecru coloured lace. Styles and patterns varied from shop to shop, giving added choice for the customer.

Dresses of cotton or crepe material were much in demand, as were items of underwear in Celanese artificial silk (pretty and decorative), although most women and girls wore the directoire style of knickers with knee elastic, the legs pullable down over the stocking tops. In our cold winters these knickers were quite a boon, especially the warmer cotton interlock ones, as stockings were not as warm as the thick tights that are worn nowadays! The over-ample female figure was kept in check with stout corsetry, mostly worn by mature ladies. Younger women wore suspender belts or a garment called a 'roll-on', the earlier examples of which stretched width-ways only so that they rode up whenever the wearer did any bending or stretching. This was an infuriating characteristic, and the advent of the 'two way stretch' came as a considerable relief.

Most women wore an apron or overall made of flowered cotton to go to work in or for working around the house. This prevented the soiling of a dress or skirt which had to be worn occasionally as a 'best', and could also be used to conceal a shabby, worn or patched garment underneath. The easily-washed synthetic materials of the present day were unknown in the 1930s and clothes had to be washed carefully then painstakingly pressed with a warm iron and wet cloth, so the 'pinnie' was a must. A good Dorcas cotton one was the best, and gave the wearer long service.

Depressed times or no, the George Street 'Woolies' had a wide range of cosmetics displayed on its counters. 'Buy Kiss-Proof Lipstick As Worn By The Stars', proclaimed the advertisements. Pond's creams, Phul-Nana face powder, Lux toilet soaps (also 'as used by the stars'), 'Evening In Paris' perfume in its familiar dark-coloured bottle, the store sold all of these. The large bottles of cologne and lavender water sold well as deodorants and as accoutrements for girls preparing to go dancing. One brand of hair shampoo came as powder in little sachets. Perhaps we did not mix it properly, but we found this to be a rather dubious preparation, turning dark hair a couple of shades lighter! Few possessed jewellery, although I did on one occasion (perhaps a birthday) manage to buy my mother a bead necklace which she liked very much. It came from Woolworth's and I paid threepence for it!

Men's suits were available at Hepworth's the 'Fifty Bob Tailors' in George Street, but although £2 10s. was very a reasonable price for a suit, it was still out of the question for the many men for whom it amounted to more than a week's pay. New suits were therefore rather uncommon. For the latest in trousers, young men chose flannel bags (known simply as 'flannels'), rather shapeless affairs measuring 24 inches at the bottom of the leg.

Fashions for the younger man were also influenced by the cinema during the early 1930s. If the General Strike of 1926 caused a furore in this country, nothing happened in 1920s Britain that was quite on a par with the introduction in America of Prohibition, which was brought into effect at the beginning of the decade and lasted for 14 years. The open warfare between rival groups of bootleggers in Chicago and New York is now looked back upon with great fascination, but at the time we took little interest in reports of events occurring thousands of miles away. During the last few years of Prohibition, however, those distant happenings were made more of a reality for us via the cinema. The talkies, when they appeared in 1929, made the perfect vehicle for the rattling sub-machine gun and the screeching tyre, and such productions as 'Scarface' and 'Public Enemy' introduced us to the film mogul's portrayal of the gangster.

It was all still very remote from everyday life, though, and if by that time America's theme song was 'Buddy, Can You Spare a Dime', we had no dimes to spare either. It was not what gangsters did that made the most immediate impression on our film-hungry cinema audiences; it was what they wore – the classic gangster outfit of black coat, white silk scarf and

Trilby hat. Perhaps not many in our area could afford the coats and silk scarves, but virtually overnight hats became very fasionable for men. Trilbys (sometimes known as 'Paddy hats' or 'soft hats') sold like hotcakes. In Aberdeen, the young men who sported them called them for some obscure reason 'down-the-river' hats. To look down from a height on a crowd of men was like looking at a sea of headgear, and hatters must have rubbed their hands in glee at this new trend. Young men as they 'walked the mat' learned to tip their hats romantically to the girls. Older men clung to the cloth cap, but everywhere could be seen variations of the trilby, or whatever the name one chose to call it.

Boys of fourteen just out of school and leaving the short trouser era behind for 'langers' (a very important event in any lad's life) longed to wear hats, but were considered too young. Hats were for their much older peers of at least sixteen or seventeen! The craze turned out to be a passing one, and eventually only more mature men persisted with it. Brilliantined hair became once again 'the latest' for the more youthful.

For young children, the standard undergarment was combinations ('combies'), a kind of union suit made of fleece-lined cotton of pink wool. It buttoned at the front and had short sleeves and thigh-length legs. Most girls wore a liberty bodice, also made of fleece-lined cotton, but sleeveless and reaching to the waist. These were warm clothes, but they would not be very popular with the children of today, used to their much more practical and sensible tights and jogging suits.

Local authority demands for the wearing of school uniforms fell mostly on deaf ears, as few families (especially large ones) could afford such things. My mother managed to provide us with gym slips, black woollen stockings, green or navy blue jumpers and navy blue knickers, but during the summer holidays she economised by making frocks for myself and my sister, run up from cotton purchased from Raggie Morrison's or Cameron's at about 6d. per yard. During one summer holiday there was a fashion for the wearing of dungarees by both girls and boys, although this did not go down so well with the boys, who preferred shorts in the warm weather. My sojourn in dungarees did not survive a report that my mother received from a neighbour concerning an outing by myself and my chums to the Links to put up tents. Made of sacking and a few long pieces of wood, these 'tenties' were only poor imitations of the real thing, but we still had to knock the uprights into the grass with a heavy stone. This lead to bruised fingers, and for a while the air was full of Anglo-Saxon, familiar to us all but seldom used by boys let alone the girls. On that occasion, however, the girls joined in the swearing (after all, weren't we like the boys, dressed up in our dungarees?) and when my mother heard of it, that was the end – the dungarees were confiscated!

Furniture was available on easy terms from the many George Street shops that sold it, but if payments were not met the goods were very quickly taken back. There were some families who never seemed to have the same set of furniture for very long! Most people who could spare a few shillings a week had a credit or 'tick' man, an agent who was sent around even the less prosperous areas to tout for credit accounts with the shop that he represented.

Over in the Castlegate, the history of the once-popular Timmer Market, held at the old Market Stance every August up to 1934, is said to stretch back to mediaeval times. The market was full of stalls selling toys, rolling pins, tattie chappers, and all manner of other articles made from sturdy white wood. It also included candy and fruit stalls, the smell of these goodies adding to the already exciting atmosphere. After dark, open carbide lamps hissed by each stall, giving cheery brightness to a market place packed with people eager to look around and to spend a few pence. Teenagers would chase each other with feather dusters on which the boys had sprinkled pepper to make the girls sneeze – all simple, innocent fun in a festivity only equalled by Hogmanay. Old and young all loved a 'walk roon the Timmerer', and we would sing:
'The morn's Timmer Market
Will a' be dressed in blue.
A blue ribbon roon' wir neck,
An' a sweetie in wir mou''
The Castlegate's weekly Friday market was unique in being mainly for the sale of second-hand goods. These came in such quantity and quality that not only Aberdonians but visitors too would take a bargain-hunting 'walk roon the Castler'. Bric-a-brac, tools of all kinds, cast-off clothing from the better off, boots and shoes, bedding, the market offered goods which few of their buyers could ever have afforded new. It took up quite a large area, and people could meet and chat in the comfort of its space. At Co-op 'divi' time it was particularly crowded, despite the necessity of channelling most of the 'divi' towards rents.

Every Saturday, a market was held at which were sold mainly sweets. For a penny we could obtain there a bag of 'chippit' fruit – damaged apples, pears, plums, etc. with the bad pieces cut out. A penny would also buy from Mitchell and Muill's at the top of Justice Street a generous bag of 'brokeners'. These were wafer biscuits of the layered kind with sweet icing filling – great for taking to Saturday matinees at the Starrie. In those days, biscuits were sold loose from deep tins with glass lids. The constant foraging in these tins by customers always resulted in a residue of broken pieces, much to the benefit of such children as ourselves!

CHAPTER 7
ON INTO THE 1930s

My grandmother's daily newspaper often contained reports of London society debutantes' seasons and presentations to Royalty at Court. Also frequently reported on were legal proceedings for breach of promise, the result of hurt pride and broken promises of marriage among the upper classes. Not that Grandmother bought the paper because of these – her main idea was to save the coupons which were printed in it, in exchange for which she received a book. The world of high society was so far removed from our own that it meant little to us.

Just as remote was the political chaos in Germany during the 1920s and early 1930s, and the ominous emergence of the Nazis. The news of Hitler's coming to power in February 1933 caused little sensation among the people of St Clements. We, as children, knew next to nothing about it, and although in the course of the decade we became increasingly aware of events outwith our country, we could still never have guessed what havoc 'Der Führer' would wreak on the world. Before that came the Spanish Civil War, in which German and Italian air power was exercised against the unfortunate Spanish Republicans; we were later to realise that this had been a mere dress rehearsal for things to come.

Fascism reared its head in Britain and was in some ways encouraged by the 'upper classes', but it gained remarkably little support among the general populace. Sir Oswald Moseley (founder of the British Union Of Fascists) and his 'blackshirts' caused near-riots at their public meetings, while in Aberdeen similar scenes attended the activities of Moseley's local counterpart, a North East laird by the name of William Chambers-Hunter. At a meeting beside the John Lewis shipyards in Torry, Chambers-Hunter's speakers were shouted down, and coal and stones thrown at them. The police had to intervene to control the angry crowds at city centre meetings, so vehemently did Aberdonians resist the intrusion. It was a common attitude that Germany and Italy were far-off foreign countries from whose deeds and opinions Britain, the tight little island, remained aloof. With a large navy to guard her shores, Brittania ruled the waves. It was forgotten that with shipbuilding at a standstill our merchant fleet was becoming old and rusty, with atrocious working conditions for its crews.

Not that local Fascists missed out on propaganda tricks. Some children were coerced into shouting 'Vote for Gow', a candidate who was attempting to make himself known in the movement. At one point an offer of 6d. was made by certain shopkeepers in the St Clement district to some of the boys to put a 'Vote for Gow' placard on their Guy Fawkes barrow when out collecting for bonfire night. No doubt the bribe was happily accepted!

Such was the background against which, in 1934, and with the eleven-plus examination (that dreaded 'qually') out of the way, I graduated along with most of my class to pastures new at Frederick Street School. Opened in 1905 with some 700 pupils, this was rather a handsome and unusual building with a playground on its flat roof. It fulfilled an important function in the secondary education of children from Hanover Street, King Street and St. Clement Street Schools. In such a densely-populated area there was no dearth of pupils, and the filtering effect of the eleven-plus made the teachers' job rather easier.

The building's stone stairways and passages echoed with the sound of many feet, especially when the 'floating' class moved around. These 'floaters' used vacated classrooms when the pupils were at P.T., sewing, art, cookery, etc – a system that worked well in this crowded establishment. For the first time we had separate classrooms for boys and girls, an arrangement apparently deemed wise for young adolescents. I have no recollection of the belt ever being administered in the girls' classes, although naturally I cannot vouch for the boys! No longer did we see irate parents calling at the classroom door demanding to know why their offspring had been given the belt. Such scenes had been quite common at primary school, and the language from some of those angry wifies was enough to turn the air blue.

Our register teacher, Miss Maitland, taught us maths. She was a well-built, sturdy lady who wore the usual long-sleeved overall, heavy stockings and 'sensible' shoes. Although severe of expression at times, she was pleasant and a very good teacher. Miss Cook taught my favourite and best subject, English. She was grey-haired, slim and energetic, dressed always in neat skirt and twin-set. She took us into the intricacies of grammar and deeper into reading, but even more fascinating were her stories of trips to France and Canada, travelling the Rocky Mountains in a glass-roofed train. We sat spellbound as she described these adventures to us in graphic detail, and we learned a great deal about places on the big wall map that she unrolled in front of the blackboard. Miss Cook never had any trouble in holding her young audiences, who were very fond of her. Women teachers in those days were all unmarried (this seems to have been required under the terms of their employment contract), and it still sounds strange to me when I hear children speak of their teachers as 'Mrs.'

While the boys had woodwork and science lessons, the girls were occupied with domesticity. Sewing class on the top floor was always fun; we had two teachers, elderly ladies who were easy to work for. Art, embroidery and various other subjects were taught by a young, tall, blonde lady named Miss Wright. Cookery lessons entailed a 'crocodile' to nearby Hanover Street School as we had no kitchen facilities of our own. Hanover Street School had a large room containing a number of gas cookers and well-scrubbed wooden tables. All the necessary equipment was available for our instruction in the making of sponge, pastry, etc. I rather shone in culinary art, not so much for pastry-making (actually my sponge was better!) but for my ability in breaking eggs into bowls without dropping them on the floor. This knack was not universally shared – I had to help several of my classmates by breaking their eggs for them. Scrubbing the tables after the lesson came naturally, as most of us scrubbed stairs at home and I had been earning my regular shilling from our neighbour in return for this service for some time. Similarly, we all showed aptitude at laundry-work and ironing!

Every fortnight came a compulsory visit to the Spray Baths at Hanover Street School, another welcome break in our classroom routine. A common room was set aside as a changing-room, and there we would disrobe to our vests and navy knickers before trooping, with our towels, through to the shower area. To preserve modesty the cubicles there were curtained and we were each given, of all things, a full length rubber apron together with a thin rubber mob-style shower cap. These caps, being of pure rubber (no nylon or polyester then), were very difficult to manoeuvre, and tended to be left perched drunkenly on our heads. The aprons might have been more effective in maintaining propriety if they had not been icy cold to touch. As soon as the janitor turned the tap on we dashed across to the showers with aprons held at arm's length, squealing whenever chill rubber touched skin! Laughing and joking, we would luxuriate in the warm water, scrubbing ourselves with the brushes and tiny pieces of soap with which we had been provided. The place was kept spotlessly clean and disinfected, and we thought a shower there wonderful.

I loved every minute of the two years that I spent at Frederick Street School, with its very wide curriculum. We had advanced from primary school children to adolescents, and were treated as such, although biology was still not taught and we had to arrive at our own conclusions (or non-conclusions) regarding the birds and the bees. This subject was the matter of much conjecture, with no help at all from our spinster lady teachers. In the home it was still taboo, and we learned nothing from the cinema, with its strict film censorship which went as far as decreeing that no double beds could be shown in bedroom scenes, and that actors' feet had always to remain on the floor in love scenes!

Religious education consisted of a passage from the Bible and a prayer at the start of the day, then on with the lessons. A few of the better essay writers were chosen from throughout the school to enter 'League Of Nations' and 'Lifeboat' essay contests. Such was the proficiency of our Miss Cook that I won three volumes of Charles Dickens novels for the former and a scrolled certificate for the latter. These were presented to me on prize-giving day along with two books for prowess at arithmetic – I suspect that Miss Maitland had relented and awarded me the latter for effort!

At this time a boy from Cotton Street named Harry Elrick enjoyed some fame at Frederick Street School thanks to his musician brother who had 'made good' in London where he had formed his own band. On the band's visits to Aberdeen, long queues formed outside His Majesty's Theatre to see George Elrick, the Aiberdeen loon who had made his native city proud of him. Later, 'Mrs Elrick's wee son George' would be the breezy, popular compère of the BBC radio programme 'Housewives' Choice', and after that a well-known impresario.

Shortly before I left St Clements Street School, I left Links Street. The increasing size of our family, which now numbered five (it would eventually number eight), necessitated a move to more spacious premises, and these were found at No. 1 Church Street. The move was arranged by negotiating an exchange with the previous tenant, Mrs Jean Welsh, who had one child, and for whose needs our smaller Links Street flat was much more suitable. Apparently the landlord at Church Street had no objection to a fairly large family moving into his property – a view not shared by many landlords, but our rent was always paid on time and I suppose he was well enough satisfied. Our new house had only two rooms, but the bedroom (at the front of the house) was quite large compared with the tiny bedroom at Links Street. It could hold a bed-settee and a bookcase as well as the usual full-size bed. The bedroom window faced the harbour, or at least that part of Waterloo Quay that was not obscured from view by the large cattlecake warehouse virtually next door.

It was the usual practice for private landlords such as ours to do relatively little by way of improvements, relying instead on the services of any resident handyman who could paint and generally maintain standards. My father painted the staircase of the Church Street house, and also put on the stairs a covering of linoleum from our old house. This was a refinement that I welcomed, as I still had the cleaning to do! There was only one other flat on our landing, that of an elderly lady, Mrs Mackie – a friendly soul who suffered from arthritis and had great difficulty in carrying out stair-cleaning chores, so I took over her turn of the stairs, which earned me a shilling a time. Her flat was beautifully clean and the furniture highly polished. When she went to visit her daughter she would give me the key so that I could keep the house dusted and fresh. When I had finished my work there I loved to sit with a book in the peace and quiet, rocking gently in her lovely old rocking chair. I earned a further shilling by going back to Links Street to clean stairs for Jean Craib; many girls had to do work like this in order to get by.

I think Grandmother must have enjoyed wash-days, as she often came to Church Street to help with the washing, of which there was always plenty, but hard work was her recipe for good health, and she should have been an authority on that. She would tell us how, during her days at the herring, she could gut fish more quickly than a German machine that was being tried out!

There were only three blocks of houses in Church Street, and across the road was Waterloo goods yard and shed. The area was a fairly quiet one apart from the times when engines and wagons rumbled along a single track which ran down the middle of the street, connecting the harbour with the gas and chemical works. By day they moved slowly, but at night they fairly shook the buildings around them.

In the tenement block next to the school was the Ancient Bar, an old establishment as its name suggests. It was little more than a rather spartan room with a bar counter, but it did have a couple of booths with tables and seating, which was unusual for an Aberdeen pub in those days. The counter was of dark wood, and had the usual brass foot rail and spittoons, or cuspidors. It was a friendly place, run efficiently by a young man named Billy.

Above the pub lived the Main family, a large brood consisting of adults except for the youngest daughter Bunty, who became my chum. Bunty was something of a tomboy, and good fun to be with. Her widowed mother was a cheery woman who ruled the household in an easy, amicable manner and never seemed to let the cares and worries of the time get her down. Every Saturday night she and a woman friend would sit in the bar, conversing over a glass of stout. In those days, pubs were not considered to be suitable places for women, but Mrs Main knew the bar staff, and was known to the regulars as being from the house upstairs.

Before going down to the bar for her weekly treat, Mrs Main would always make the Sunday broth in her large black cooking pot. The vegetables would be bought from Hunter's at the top of Church Street, and the soup would be left to simmer slowly all Saturday night. Often on a Sunday I would sit at the table with Bunty, enjoying a plate of broth into which had been put a large spoonful of creamed potatoes – 'Hiv some chappit tatties!' The Mains' house was much like anyone else's in those hard-up days, with bare lino floors and perhaps a small rug or mat at the fireplace, which was a black and steel affair with side oven. My grandmother slaved most mornings cleaning and emery-papering her own grate, and would have frowned at the state of many others, but grates like these were monstrosities to keep, and demanded considerable strength and dedication to the task!

I tried to interest Bunty in the Girls Guildry, but to no avail. I went there regularly, dressed in my white blouse, navy blue skirt, red sash, and navy blue bowl-shaped hat. I had a chum there too, a girl named Dorothy who lived in St Clement Street. Her mother was a widow, and worked as a cleaner. After a walk to the beach on a Sunday, I would often be invited back to their house for tea and some delicious home-made date loaf. Dorothy's two brothers were accomplished ballroom dancers, and before long they began instructing us in this social grace. As a child, I had been packed off along with my sister Margaret to Highland dancing classes, ably run by Madame Watson who lived in Commerce Street. This instruction cost mother 1s. an hour, or 5d. each for two. Madame Watson had a large number of pupils, many of whom appeared in dancing displays. We progressed gradually from Highland to ballet dancing, and my mother bought us ballet shoes and made us dresses for displays. Many excellent dancers were produced by Madame Watson, but unfortunately neither my sister nor myself were in that category, and eventually we gave up, although we never forgot the steps that we learned.

Ballroom dancing had become very popular at the turn of the 1930s, the black bottom and the charleston of the 1920s having given place to the foxtrot and the quickstep, although the waltz remained as much of a favourite as ever. The recently-built Beach Ballroom, with its enormous sprung dance floor and central island fountain and banks of plants, was an ideal place to go, especially as public transport was available at all hours to take dancers home. At 1.30 a.m. Corporation tramcars would be lined up outside, and for only a few coppers more than the daytime rate it was possible to travel from there to most destinations in the city. Women in long evening dresses could be seen entering the ballroom for 'special' dances held by such organisations as swimming clubs or cricket clubs, or through the combined effort of the tradesmen of the city in arranging an annual jamboree. Soft drinks and coffee were served in the gallery upstairs.

Dorothy and I made enthusiastic dancing pupils. Most of our lessons took place at Jimmy Donald's ballroom in North Silver Street. We were nearly fourteen, the end of school was imminent, and many of our age group were given parental approval to go to this very respectable and well run hall – but to there only. No nonsense was tolerated in the ballroom, and strict rules had to be observed. In particular the floor was barred to 'trucking', the latest 'pop' dance step, in which the feet were shuffled in time to the music while a finger was waved in the air. One boy was asked to leave the floor after he nonchalantly attempted to scan the football scores in the Evening Express as he danced with his partner! So successful were our tutors that Dorothy and I bypassed the learners' class and went straight to the public dances upstairs.

We did bend parental rules just a little by trying out the Red Triangle, in the Loyal Order Of Ancient Shepherds' hall above the Cinema House, entered from No. 42 Union Terrace. There was a good band there and a young crowd who were keen dancers like ourselves. It was great fun, and soon we were learning to make ourselves look fashionable as well. This entailed much experimenting with the hair-tongs, and gave rise to several episodes with singed hair and burned fingers, but with all the vanity of the young we carried on regardless.

Saturday night dancing ended for me (temporarily, at least) when my father forbade it on the grounds that I was too young. Also my mother was concerned that the luxury of a shilling a week and a supply of 7d. pairs of stockings from the Equitable was too much for the family finances. I would have to wait until I left school and found a job, so it was back to ankle socks and fourpence for the Starrie on Friday nights, the Saturday 'tuppenny rush' having been outgrown.

We had one very enjoyable dance in the church hall, organised by the senior Girls Guildry and the Boys Brigade. There was a band consisting of piano, accordion and drums, the drums being played by our minister the Rev. R.R. Robertson, who showed quite some prowess in keeping the dance tunes to a strict tempo. I think he enjoyed the evening as much as the dancers did.

Mr Robertson was popular with the young folk at the church for his friendly and outgoing nature, and his ability to mingle with his 'flock' at any social occasion. His preaching was often dramatic and was always interesting, his voice carrying clearly around the church and his arms often raised to emphasise a point. I vaguely remember his predecessor, a tall thin young man named Jenkins, who even when visiting wore very formal clothes and carried a 'lum' hat. Mr Robertson arrived in 1932 and stayed until 1947 when he moved to Foveran.

From time to time, foreign naval destroyers would berth at Waterloo Quay. Germans and Frenchmen were frequent visitors, and it was fascinating to see all the different uniforms. On Sundays the public was allowed on board to view the ships, and, in the company of adults, most of the local children clambered over the grey-painted vessels. Sailors on shore leave usually frequented the nearest pubs and dance hall, the latter being the Plaza in the former St Clement's Episcopal Church, Prince Regent Street. The Ancient Bar was often packed with sailors, the locals managing to commandeer the seats and tables while still making the foreigners feel welcome! Sailors seemed to have a particular bent for walking up and down the middle of Church Street rather than on the pavement – perhaps they felt safer there! Heavy motor traffic had yet to come, and in Church Street all that had to be avoided was the occasional goods train.

The London boat set sail from the harbour on Saturday midnight one week and midday the next, depending on the tide, and during my time in Church Street I was taken one night to watch her leave. Accompanied by Bunty Main and her older brother, we watched the passengers board the

Young visitors make the most of their visit on board a destroyer.

Queues of curious Aberdonians also visited the vessel.

ship, the *City Of London*. Bathed in the glow of lights, it was an exciting scene as people stood on the quay to see off their friends and relations. When all passengers and their luggage had embarked, the ship's siren sounded deeply and loudly, and she smoothly moved off to begin her journey to the far-off capital.

At this point a local man, three sheets to the wind and happy with it, struck up with the old Harry Lauder song

'*So we parted on the shore,*
Yes we parted on the shore,
I said 'Goodbye, love, I'm off to Baltimore'.
Then I kissed her on the cheek and the crew began to roar,
Heeley-ho! Heeley-ho!' and we parted on the shore'.

A strangely fitting send-off to a lovely ship.

Just as in any sea-port, the dockland area had its quota of prostitutes plying their trade on the quays. 'Ladies of the night', call them what you will, to the local people they were the 'shorewalkers', and many of them were known and recognised by the older children of the area. The favoured term was 'They ging wi' men', and vaguely we knew that they provided some kind of service. They did us no harm, and were accepted as part of life.

Among those ladies the most notable was the famous 'Snuffy Ivy' – a legend in her own lifetime, and known throughout the city. Her nickname came about through an impediment of speech which made her words emerge with a strange nasal sound. Jokes about her were legion, the teller guying her distinctive voice; one that went the rounds was 'He gave me half-a-croon then hid the chick t' ask for some change back!' Ivy, it should be stated, gave considerable sums of money to charity over the years, although she never rose from her poor background. Latterly she lived in quiet obscurity, but she was not forgotten. Her death a few years ago was accorded prominent reports in the local press.

The summer of 1936 arrived, and our class at Frederick Street School prepared to say goodbye to the teachers who in two crowded years had done their best to equip us to face the outside world. Just before we left, we went on a class trip to Edinburgh. This was an exciting adventure for those whose parents could scrape together 9s., payable in weekly instalments. I was a little blasé about the trip, as I had already travelled to Glasgow by train. An aunt from the paternal side of the family had visited us on an 8s. day excursion, and had taken myself and a friend back with her for a few days. My friend and I were so homesick that we were sent back again, and I think my aunt was glad to see the back of us, but that was now conveniently forgotten. This time I was older and thoroughly enjoyed the trip. Arriving in Edinburgh, we covered a great deal of ground. We visited Binns, the large Princes Street store, where out of my 1s. pocket money I paid 7d. for a pink face cloth to take home to mother. This was followed by visits to the castle and the Zoo. It was a fine day, the trip was grand, and it was a tired but happy party that arrived back at the Joint Station that night. In those days it was not British Rail that took us over the Forth Bridge but L.M.S., as railway companies were still private and separate.

The employment situation being what it was, Bunty and I took some time to find work, so a few weeks after leaving school we and a few friends set out with some sandwiches on an open-front tram, bound for Hazlehead. There, Bunty assured us, we could make money by picking berries in the fruit orchards. As we walked along the dusty road we saw the berry pickers at work. Bunty called 'Any jobs, mister?', and a man who was obviously the gaffer told us to 'jump the dyke'. We picked black currants and put them in baskets which were weighed when full. For each full basket we received some coppers. The sun was warm, the smell of the fruit pleasant, and we worked steadily until 5 o'clock, when it was time to catch the tram home. Some of us felt a little queasy, as we had been eating berries despite being forbidden to do so by the gaffer, although his concern was more for the profits of the fruit orchard than for our health!

Each morning we boarded the Hazlehead 'carrie', arriving for work at 8 a.m. The bushes were thick with fruit, and there was plenty of work to do. When thirst overtook us in the sun (which it frequently did) we took drinks from lemonade bottles of water, declaring ourselves 'ploatin' in the warm airlessness. Overtime was offered, so our little group found itself weeding long rows of strawberries and small flowering plants, which necessitated a great deal of kneeling. 'It's afa' raxin'' was the general moan as limbs and backs began to ache, but the thought of perhaps a pound at the end of the week spurred us on. We worked a long day until 8 p.m., and it was a tired and dusty group that boarded the tram each evening. Excitement mounted as pay-day approached, not only on our part but also on that of our mothers, who more than welcomed any extra earnings to put towards home finances.

The eagerly-awaited time came, and the gaffer handed each of us a small envelope, inside which we found the princely sum of 7s. 6d. – 37½ pence! Instantly, there was pandemonium. 'It's a swick!' 'A' that work for seven an' six?' 'Ploatin' in the heat an' raxin' wir backs for that?' The enjoyment of our days in the sun was forgotten – and what would our mothers say? Our protests only earned us the sack, the gaffer choosing a few choice expletives with which to send us on our way. As we quickly walked back to the road we spotted rhubarb growing in plenty, and some large beds of cutting flowers. Revenge! We filled our arms with as much of both as we could carry and dashed like the wind for the tram, laughing at our escape as we rumbled into the distance.

After the berry picking fiasco, Bunty and I spent much of our time child-minding, taking kids to the beach where we let them paddle in the sea, build sandcastles, etc, and for our troubles we received enough coppers to pay for our Friday nights at the Starrie. Cleaning jobs continued, of course, and one Saturday morning when I had finished the stairs and assured my mother that no caddis (fluff) was left under the beds or other furniture, Bunty and I set off for the jetty at Pocra Quay, armed with scrubbing brushes, cloths and Brasso. Our purpose was to clean my uncle Andrew's boat *Daisy* in readiness for an afternoon's fishing in the bay, to which Bunty and I had been invited. We pulled in the boat from where it lay among the other small craft, boarded it, and soon had it clean and shining for Andrew and his pals. The trip to the bay was fine, but when the fishing began and we lay beam on to the slight swell, we girls began to enjoy ourselves rather less. Soon we became violently sea-sick, but the boys fished on and we were very thankful when at last the boat headed back to the jetty. Once on shore, Bunty and I vowed never to set foot in a boat again, even to clean it!

I recollect that when Andrew and his pals returned from these summer fishing trips in the *Margaret* or the *Daisy* they would come back to Links Street with not only a few fish but also a ravenous appetite. So each week my Grandmother made them a dumpling. It was not exactly a rich fruit 'clootie', but it did have a handful of raisins in it. It consisted of pieces of bread, left-over scones, etc, boiled inside a white dumpling cloth in the large cooking pot. When ready it was taken out, put on a plate and left in front of the fire to dry out a little and form an outer skin. The boys ate it all, referring to it as 'the sinker'. One of the lads, who had a keen sense of humour, remarked, 'It's just as weel we eat the dumpling after we've been oot in the boatie, otherwise, the boatie would sink!' And it was just as well that Granny also had a sense of humour. The term 'sinkers' was also applied to doughballs, so it was 'tatties, mince and sinkers' for dinner or for supper on some days (we never spoke of 'lunch' or 'tea'), and even when the doughballs were cooked to a delicious lightness they were still 'sinkers'!

The child-minding continued. 'We'll tak' any age', we would tell mothers, 'Even bairns in hippens' (nappies), and so we pushed prams to the beach as well as accompanying walking children. 'Dinna pick the pee-the-beds', we warned the latter, as there was a popular superstition that any child bringing home dandelions would wet the bed at night. Our seat in the Starrie was well earned, and business was good enough for us to position ourselves near the exits in order to effect a quick getaway when the audience stood for 'God Save The King' at the end of the show, so that a walk around the Beach Carnival could be fitted in to round off our evening.

There were plenty of other things to do. I paid frequent visits to Aunt Daisy, especially as she had just purchased one of the new cabinet gramophones. This impressive piece of furniture, French polished with a rich dark finish, was viewed by us with some awe. On it I first heard the popular song of the time 'Marquitta', which I thought beautiful and romantically haunting. On my occasional baby-sitting visits I liked to take out the record and play it to myself. My chums pronounced Aunt Daisy's house 'afa' posh' – we even had evaporated milk in the tea!

Edmand & Spark At last I found a job. Armed with a green card from the juvenile Broo in Union Terrace, I went to a firm of printers and bookbinders in Queen Street for an interview. The clerkess looked down at me from her high desk, set in a corner next to a large window, and I could see her eyeing my best coat, neat short hair, polished shoes and white ankle socks. 'Ankle socks?', she sniffed. Not, it appears, appropriate apparel for someone seeking a job with that firm. Neverthless, a cursory glance at my school record card seemed to satisfy her, and I was told to report the following Monday. My salary was 7s.10d. per week – actually 8s., but with 2d. deducted for National Insurance. My mother was not very pleased at my receiving such a low rate of pay for the fairly long hours that I had to work, but at least the job was within easy walking distance of home so that I could return for lunch. The wage, although small, was still very welcome. I was given 2s. per week in pocket money, and also when necessary a pair of the Equitable's artificial silk stockings. So every morning I walked up Miller Street past the 'Big Hoose' (a particularly tall block of tenements), and up Commerce Street to Queen Street, in time for work at 8 a.m. An hour was given for lunch at midday, and work finished at 5.45 p.m. On Saturdays we worked from 8 a.m. until midday. Sometimes I was sent on 'trips out' – errands, for instance, to the jobbing department of Aberdeen Journals in Broad Street. The manager there, Mr Stewart, was very kind, and I thought the place very exciting and interesting.

In the course of searching for this first employment I encountered my fair share of snobbery. Employers were well able to pick and choose among candidates, especially school leavers. A good record card from school was no guarantee of success in finding employment in some shops. For them, ability to count came second to personal appearance and accent. Also, there was one subject about which it was wise to keep silent in an interview. One day I went to see the manager of a certain shop in the 'classier' category. Dressed in my smart green coat with nice covered buttons, my well-brushed brown shoes and matching handbag, I made sure to speak in 'plain English' as taught in school. I particularly avoided saying such things as 'off of', which to Miss Cook was dreadful grammar and which we now hear regularly from Americans! But everything went wrong when I ventured to enquire what the salary would be. A cold, aloof expression appeared on the manager's face and I knew that I was not going to be a successful applicant. Money was not, seemingly, supposed to be important. However, I learned from the experience, and while I may have been wearing ankle socks when I obtained my job in Queen Street, I certainly never raised the matter of wages! During my days at Queen Street, I became friendly with a girl, Violet, who worked in a baker's shop farther along the street. We would meet up at the corner of St Nicholas Street where Queen Victoria's statue then stood. 'Meet you at the Queen' was a common phrase among younger Aberdonians, for whom this was a favourite rendezvous point. Violet lived with her granny in an old tenement house in the town centre, and worked very long hours. She had to rise very early to begin work at 6 a.m. each day, and all for £1 a week.

One Sunday I was invited for tea, and afterwards sat chatting. I must have overstayed my welcome, as at about 8.30p.m. Violet stood up, quickly undressed to her underwear, turned down the gas light and jumped into the kitchen bed, bidding me 'Goodnight, see you tomorrow!' As I let myself out I felt somewhat bemused that anyone should be going to bed so early, but then I did not have to work such a very long day! Without doubt, we were locked into a class system that imposed such long hours and low pay. With so many unemployed, and with people queuing at the backs of those that were working, whatever their pay and conditions, there was little choice for the likes of Violet. She was a cheerful warm-hearted girl, and we remained good chums until I changed my job and moved from Queen Street.

Being now 14 years of age and a wage-earner, I found many new horizons opening to me on the social scene, including entitlement to Saturday night dancing. I had the great pleasure of going to my first staff dance, for which my father bought me my first evening dress. It cost a guinea from a small fashion shop in George Street, and was made of lovely pale green taffeta. I sold tickets for the dance to some of the young lads who worked at Aberdeen Journals, with whom I had become acquainted in the course of my employment. The venue was the Bon Accord Hotel in Market Street, the band was good, and I spent a wonderful evening.

There were many dance halls to choose from, dancing having by now become the favourite recreation for Aberdeen's younger set, although the cinema still remained extremely popular – by this time prices in the newer cinemas averaged 1s. for available seats, queuing at 9d. and Balcony at 1s.9d., but the smaller houses charged much less, and the Starrie and Casino still sufficed for the people of our area. Saturday night dancing at St Katherine's Club in West North Street cost only 9d. The club had a cafe which sold tea and soft drinks, and anyone willing to help serve these during the interval was admitted free. My current chum and I willingly volunteered, thus saving 9d. out of our meagre pocket money to spend at the cinema during the week. I never went to Nell Beaton's popular dance

A 'Co-op' bike for £3-19-6! This was a great deal of money for most folk in 1933.

Flat bonnets to the fore! A Cup-tie crowd at Pittodrie watch as the Dons comprehensively beat Dumbarton 6-1.

hall in the Gallowgate, but Georgie and his pals did. Georgie also tried the Plaza in Prince Regent Street, but told us that he found it 'a bit rough'. I suspect this to have been the understatement of the year. I went with some of the girls from work to the Abergeldie Ballroom in the Hardgate, where we danced to an excellent band called the Embassy Six. Bands which did not maintain strict tempo were very heavily criticised, but Aberdeen sported many that could satisfy the most discerning of dancers. Wiseman's Rooms in Spring Garden held dances, but most often these took the form of private functions with a 2s or 2s.6d. admission charge, and demanded the formality of long evening dresses.

No trouble was caused by alcoholic drink at dance halls; most people were lucky to be able to afford admission and a soft drink. Halls had no liquor licences at that time, and we never missed them. For our elders, tea or coffee and a sandwich was enough of a treat at their whist drives or 'Copie Guildies'.

The rest of our leisure time was enjoyed to the full in healthy activities. We wore out the heels of countless pairs of shoes with regular walks to the beach (even on stormy Sundays) or, in the fine summer days, to the parks where we could have drinks of cold water from the granite cups chained to the fountains. Later, a cycling fad hit the city and hordes of young folk headed out of town on Sundays. Standard dress for girls was corduroy shorts and short matching jacket, and thus equipped we went on cycle 'rallies' to such places as Potarch. At least to begin with it was my pals that went – I had to wait until I found a new job at a larger wage before my mother brought home an Elswick sports bike, for which she paid by small weekly instalments. She was by then employed for a couple of days each week at the Kittybrewster Mart Café, making the payments possible.

And there was football. The terraces of Aberdeen's football ground at Pittodrie were regularly packed with enormous crowds which converged on foot or by tram to cheer on the home team (it was hoped) to victory. The crowd swayed and surged forward during the more exciting moments, but behaviour was generally orderly, although from time to time loudly-voiced opinions could be heard on individual team members, or more often the referee and his antecedents. People who loved the game (it has always been a passion of mine) admired the skill and grace of the best footballers, and soccer violence was not known. 'Come awa' the Dons' was the cry, and the joy when the home team won made the match worth every penny of the admission charge. The game would be the subject of conversation and debate for many days after.

Union Street on Sunday evenings was always thronged with young folk who, having spent most of their pocket money the previous night, paraded up and down the thoroughfare in a ritual known as 'walking the mat'. From Market Street, and staying on that side of the street only, I and my chums would walk on the outside of the pavement going up and on the inside going down. This pleasant and sometimes quite exciting pastime gave more than just the opportunity of a Sunday stroll – it also offered the possibility of catching the eye of a member of the opposite sex, perhaps someone from a dance the night before, who lived too far away to be seen home or to see one home but had said 'See you at the mat'. This was cheaper than having to fork out tram fares, and in the economic conditions of the time most people understood.

Dress was strictly formal. Girls wore their good coats and shoes, and usually hats. Handbags and gloves completed our outfit. Halo hats with large upturned front brim were high fashion and were quite becoming. In the cinema they were less than welcome, causing annoyance to those sitting behind ('Tak' aff that hat – I canna see the screen!'), but when 'walking the mat' we could wear them with easy aplomb. Boys wore their best serge suits with a gaberdeine coat draped over their arm, but whatever the finery on a Sunday, come Monday we would all be back in our working clothes.

Police on duty during our mat-walking (there were two that I remember) kept a watchful eye on those who stopped to talk for too long, especially in such places as Woolies' doorway. Politely but firmly, they moved us back into the crowd. Shop-breaking could hardly have been further from our minds, but we respected the police, for whom this was merely in the line of duty. We would never have argued with them – we would have been afraid to go home if we had ended up in any trouble!

By 1938 it seemed ever surer that this hungry, anxious decade was going to end in war - a just war, many felt, against the evil of Nazism – and Fascist factions at their political meetings in the Castlegate and elsewhere found that none of their repellent philosophy would be tolerated in a country preparing to fight for democracy at any price. During this period of tension and political unrest, my St Clements days came to an end. In the autumn of 1938 our flat in Church Street was destroyed in a fire which we could only surmise to have begun with a dislodged gas poker and a nursery fireguard draped with drying clothes. We lost everything, and it was some years before the family recovered from its misfortune. For a few weeks I stayed with Mary Jane Smith in St Clement Street, but after that I left along with the rest of the family for other parts of the city.

My one-time homes in Church Street and Links Street have now vanished, as have the old community and spirit of St Clements. Passing through the area subsequently on visits to my grandparents in Fittie, I thought how little I missed its grey, narrow streets. I was no longer interested in houses without bathrooms etc, and I felt no inclination ever to live there again. But on returning to the area at intervals during the 1960s and 1970s, and seeing

Church Street in the 1970's, still with its railway lines.

St Clements Street, late 1960's. On the left, the 'Copie' shops and houses.
Further down, the gable end of the St Clements Bar.

Since this photograph was taken in the 1970's all these buildings have vanished.

Dereliction. The corner of Wellington Street some years ago. Colletta's shop is no more, but the buildings shown here have since been cleaned and restored, and are now among the few survivors.

it first empty and derelict then being obliterated altogether, I realised that I do not in any way envy the youth of today.

I grew up in one of the poorer areas of Aberdeen during the hardest years of this century, but, hackneyed though this may seem, I could have wished for no better a childhood. St Clements was a way of life. Let this book be a small memorial to it.